The **Meat Club** Cookbook
[GIRLS ONLY]

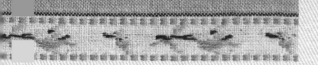

The Meat Club Cookbook
[GIRLS ONLY]

For Gals Who Love Their Meat!

By Vanessa Dina, Kristina Fuller, and Gemma DePalma
with Leslie Jonath

Illustrations by Caroline Hwang

CHRONICLE BOOKS
SAN FRANCISCO

Library of Congress Cataloging-in-Publication Data available.

ISBN 0-8118-4525-7

Manufactured in China.

Designed by *Vanessa Dina*

Distributed in Canada by Raincoast Books
9050 Shaughnessy Street
Vancouver, British Columbia V6P 6E5

10 9 8 7 6 5 4 3 2 1

Chronicle Books LLC
85 Second Street
San Francisco, California 94105

www.chroniclebooks.com

Dedication

To Mom and Gretta, my favorite girls!
—Vanessa

To my Dad, for his steadfast support,
encouragement, and belief in the Meat Club.
—Kristina

To Mom, Grams, and Marie – Three of the
most important ingredients in my life.
—Gemma

Acknowledgments

The Meat Club would like to thank Chronicle Books for believing in us. Special thanks to Bill LeBlond, our editor, for his constant support and encouragment; to Leslie Jonath, for her wicked way with words. Amy Treadwell, Jan Hughes, Doug Ogan, and Donna Linden — a fabulous team. Thanks also to Caroline Hwang, for her wonderous talents with a needle and thread and her ability to make meat look oh-so-cute! A big thanks to Frankie Whitman and Niman Ranch for their meaty support — recipe testing was a culinary delight using Niman beef, pork, and lamb! Thank you to Erica Holland-Toll, our gal-chef at Americano, for all of her tasty tips and recipes. And finally, a great big thanks to our mothers, sisters, aunties, grannies, and friends who have taught us to navigate through our kitchens and enjoy the beauty of good food, and who have contributed to our Meat Club in so many wonderful ways. We love you.

Contents
★ ★ ★

Welcome to the Club!

Are you a girl who lusts after big steaks, succulent ribs, and juicy burgers? Do you find yourself full of desire for braised lamb shanks and fork-tender pork loin? Are you usually the only girl cutting into a rare rib-eye in a sea of salad eaters? Do you long to find other women who feel the way you do? If your answer is yes, you are the ideal candidate for

The Meat Club: Girls Only.

Before starting the club, we didn't know many women who admitted to craving meat. A lunch with the girls meant a Caesar salad or a poached chicken breast. Our dinner parties were inundated with vegetarians and finicky eaters; at restaurants, we were embarrassed to order meat for fear of offending someone. Despite our enormous appetites for life, we were starved for meaty culinary adventures!

Contrary to popular opinion, meat isn't just for men. So, we decided to found a girls' meat club to reclaim possession of what is rightfully ours—guilt-free meat eating. We were three girls at different stages in our lives: one new mother, one swinging single, and one recent divorcée. The idea came to us over dinner one night when we realized our mutual secret passion. Since then, we've met once a week to share our favorite meat dishes and dish about our lives. What started as a fun idea has evolved into a relished ritual.

**The rules governing membership
in the Meat Club are simple:**

★1★

You have to be a girl.

★2★

You have to love to cook and eat meat.

★3★

You have to love to talk about meat (any kind).

★4★

What's said in the Meat Club stays in the Meat Club!

As members, we've learned more about meat than we ever imagined possible. We've debriefed our butchers. We've experimented with sauces, rubs, and marinades. We've tried out new recipes, researched other people's favorites, and made up some of our own.

Meat has also led to juicy conversations. Indeed, there is nothing better to talk about than meat, whether it's the kind you roast, braise, or even date. We've had succulent successes, but we've also been burned a few times! The *Meat Club* has become a sisterhood—a place to share our lives and our meaty tales.

Meat is healthy—especially for gals. We *Meat Club* gals strive to make healthful choices when it comes to our bodies. Grass-finished, natural, and organic meats purchased from local artisan butchers or specialty grocers have lower fat content, no preservatives or artificial ingredients, and contain essential vitamins and minerals like vitamin E and iron. In fact, the iron in beef is easier for the body to absorb than the iron present in most other foods. Like all good things in life, meat is healthiest when consumed in moderation. Once we started eating meat without guilt, we felt stronger and happier.

The *Meat Club* Cookbook is a collection of tried-and-true recipes culled from our best meals—many of them easy updated classics from our mothers and grandmothers and from other girls like us who relish good home cooking. We have divided it into chapters by type of meat, with basic information on how to choose and prepare the most popular cuts of beef, lamb, and pork. Simply put, this is a book for all you girls who want to have your meat and eat it, too.

Chapter One
Meet Your Meat

We didn't grow up eating **filet mignon** topped with creamy Gorgonzola sauce, pork tenderloin marinated in red wine, or citrus-scented Moroccan **lamb tagine.** We grew up at a time when bland '70s cuisine ruled the popular American culinary palate and the possibilities of **meat** seemed limited to pot roast and well-done steaks. Kristina's childhood version of a stir-fry included **ground beef,** onions, and American cheese, while Vanessa remembers making hot-dog goulash for her family using powdered garlic. When we started the **Meat Club,** we thought butterflies only flew in the garden and the adjective "frenched" only described an intimate kiss. In short, we were **new to meat.**

★★★

Of course, our mothers and grandmothers had their specialties, but none of us appreciated their efforts at the time and we left home without asking for the recipes. As adults, knowing how to choose and **cook meat** was completely daunting.

Even though we loved to eat steaks and chops, the prospect of shopping for the goods and cooking them right was intimidating. So many meats, so little time! What was a girl to do?

Our first encounters with meat included: 1] reading books by meat masters, 2] asking our mothers and friends for recipes and cooking tips, and 3] establishing a fulfilling committed relationship with a butcher. Even though the Meat Club has been going for years, we still learn something new with every recipe and at every meeting. No matter how much meat knowledge we've gained, happily there's always more to learn.

Whether you prefer beef, lamb, or pork, there are certain basics you should know. So now it's time to meet your meat: Get to know your butcher, learn to choose your cuts, and master the cooking methods that will guide you to meat-cooking bliss.

★ ★ ★

Your New Love: The Butcher

Married or single, a meat-loving girl's true love is her butcher. Find a good butcher and good food will follow. However, a good butcher, like a good man, can be hard to find, especially as neighborhood butcher shops have gradually given way to large supermarket chains. But don't despair if you don't have a local butcher shop. Knowledgeable people are often at work behind the meat counters in small grocery stores and many specialty stores. Seek out the best butcher you can find and then establish a deep, committed relationship.

During the winnowing process, rely on thorough but friendly interrogation techniques: Who supplies your meat? What is the grade and quality of your meat? How long has the meat been aged? How was the meat packed and shipped? Where on the animal does this cut come from? Is it a flavorful cut? How is it best prepared? A good butcher will be able to advise you on what cuts are suitable for the recipe you are cooking and even suggest substitute cuts. When you find a butcher who answers your questions and survives your interrogation with charm, don't be fickle. Loyalty is important to a future filled with good meat.

★ ★ ★

How to Buy Meat

Of course, the best way to find a good butcher is to know a little something about meat before you enter the shop. If you go prepared with some basic information, your evaluation of any potential lifelong butcher—just as in choosing a lifelong partner—will be sounder. Selecting the most flavorful piece of meat from a counter full of choices can make you dizzy, but a few tips, good for beef, lamb, or pork, will ease your anxiety. (Don't worry. We've detailed what qualities to look for in each kind of meat at the beginning of their respective chapters.) In general, you should evaluate each piece by four criteria: appearance (we know that sounds superficial, but trust us— when it comes to meat, it's important), grade, label, and supplier.

A Great Look

First and foremost, any piece of meat should look appetizing—as only a piece of raw meat can! Look not only at the color of the meat, but also at the color of the fat, which should be creamy white, rather than yellow. The color of the meat itself should be vibrant and consistent with its type: cherry red to brownish red for beef and lamb, and pale pink for pork. The texture should have a fine grain. In other words, the meat should look fresh and appealing.

Making the Grade

All meat is graded by the United States Department of Agriculture (USDA) based on the age of the animal, the amount of internal fat (marbling), and the physique of the animal (and you thought you were hard on yourself!). The terminology is different for the different kinds of animals (see pages 28, 76, and 108), but we recommend you buy the highest grade you can afford. Beware of any names on the package that sound like grades, but aren't standard, such as "butcher's choice." Such declarations are typically all about marketing, rather than meat.

Designer Labels

The names of various cuts can be confusing, often varying from one part of the country to another. This is especially true of beef and of steak in particular (see What's at Steak?, page 32). For example, the same cut is called a New York strip in Kansas City and a Kansas City strip in New York—the names may even vary from one market to another in the same city. We delve into that tangled name game later on. The label should help you to identify the primal cut, that is, the area of the animal where the meat comes from.

Specialty Brands and Suppliers

We prefer branded meat from local and specialty producers and buy our meat from regional and national suppliers whose products we trust. Companies such as Niman Ranch and Meyer Natural, who raise their animals under superior conditions, are known for the high quality of their meats. These operations also readily include ample information on the source of their meat. We recommend finding a good supplier in your area (see Resources, page 133). With a good butcher and a good supplier, you are in for good meat eating.

★ ★ ★

Natural, Organic, and Grass-Fed Meat: What Does It All Mean?

Great quality meat comes from great producers who tend to their animals with care. Most meat you find at the grocery store is raised on grain and other feed that contains added antibiotics and growth hormones. When buying meat, we highly recommend seeking out natural or organic meats that are raised on feed containing neither. We much prefer the taste and texture of natural and organic meats. They are healthier and more humane—not only for our bodies and for the animals, but for the environment.

Organic Meat

We love organic meat, but it can be pricey because of the high cost of producing it. To be certified organic, not only must the meat never be exposed to antibiotics, growth hormones, pesticides, genetically modified ingredients, or irradiation, it must be raised mostly on organic pastureland and feed. Organic meat is wonderful if you can find it at an affordable price.

Natural Meat

For our money and meat-loving cravings, we think natural meat is the way to go. Increasingly available, moderately priced, and rich in flavor, natural meat does not contain artificial flavors, coloring, ingredients, or chemical preservatives, antibiotics, or hormones, and it is minimally processed. Be aware that certain producers are more rigorous than others and it is important to get to know a producer you can trust.

Grass-Fed Meat

Most conventional meat animals start on grass and then are moved to a feedlot to feed on grain. Meat defined as "grass-fed" is fed start to finish on grass, so grass-fed meat is sometimes technically referred to as grass-finished meat. The terms grass-fed and free-range are still being defined in legal terms, so it can be quite confusing. Being labeled grass-fed does not necessarily mean that the meat is organic, and being organic doesn't mean that the meat is grass-finished. Unless the label reads, "100 percent grass-fed" or "pasture finished," the animal was most likely raised on some amount of grain. Grass-fed meat is very good for the environment and the animals and contains nutrients (from grass!), most notably omega-3 fatty acids, which are very healthful. We enjoy grass-fed meat because of its big flavor, though some would describe the meat as tougher than natural due to its lean physique and lack of fat.

To help you in your search for good meat, we've provided a list of wonderful producers in the Resources section (page 133) who provide natural, organic, and/or grass-fed meats of the highest quality.

★ ★ ★

Meaty Cooking Methods

A well-prepared dish is all about the perfect match: the right cut with the right cooking method. There are basically two types of cooking methods—quick and slow. Quick methods, best for flavorful cuts that start out tender, include broiling, grilling, pan roasting, and sautéing. Slow methods, suited to flavorful cuts that need tenderizing, include braising, roasting, and stewing.

We've often chosen cuts of meat and their respective meaty methods by how much time we have. Home early from a date and need a quick bite? Sauté a steak in just a few minutes. Need to warm up a house on a cold winter night? Consider an oven-roasted leg of lamb. As members of the Meat Club, we like to think, good times or bad times, there is always time for a nice piece of meat!

First, an important rule of thumb: Most of our recipes call for browning the meat, which boosts flavor by imparting a rich, dark color to the surface. This rich, dark color and flavor is due to the caramelized natural sugars in the meat juices. Browning is usually the first step in a cooking method, whether you are pan roasting a lamb chop or braising a beef shank. But sometimes it's the whole recipe, such as when you're quickly searing a pork cutlet. Once you come to appreciate the flavor browning imparts, you'll want to brown nearly every piece of meat.

Two more rules of thumb involve room temperature and resting. Many recipes call for bringing the meat to room temperature before it hits the fire, to ensure even cooking. Otherwise you could end up with a hot exterior and a cold core. Then, when most meats are done, it is equally important to let them rest anywhere from five to twenty minutes before serving, for a more uniformly juicy result. Juices are automatically forced to the center of a piece of meat during cooking, so letting your roast or other cut put its feet up for a while once it's away from the fire gives those same juices time to redistribute themselves throughout the meat.

The degree of doneness is up to you. Every meat lover's kitchen needs an instant-read thermometer (see page 24) for testing, of course. In each chapter, we've provided a list of temperatures with approximate times for rare, medium-rare, medium, and well-done meat. No two stoves or cooks are alike, so keep in mind that these are only guidelines, until you determine the idiosyncrasies of both of you. Now, on to the methods, in easy-to-navigate alphabetical order.

Braising

Slow and easy, braising can be your best friend when you want to transform a tough cut into a tender one. Technically speaking, braising is cooking relatively large cuts of meat in a small amount of liquid (if the meat is completely submerged and the pieces are smaller, you are stewing). Braising is a great make-ahead method when you are entertaining, as it allows for lots of conversation before the meal. The best cuts for braising are tough or fatty roasts (brisket, bottom round, lamb shoulder, and the like), meaty ribs of every guise (often finished on a grill or under a broiler), and stocky shanks.

Basic Braising: Pat the meat dry, then generously season with salt and pepper and dust with flour. In a heavy pot, heat oil over high heat and brown the meat on all sides to form a flavorful crust. If you are adding any aromatics (diced carrot, celery and onion, and herbs), remove the meat and sauté them in the oil until they are caramelized. Return the meat to the pot, add liquid (stock, wine, beer) to immerse the meat halfway, bring to a simmer, cover, and cook until tender on the stove top or in a moderate oven (350°F). Depending on the cut and size of the meat, this can take an hour or two. Once the meat is done, you can make a sauce by reducing the cooking liquid and serving it as is, or adding butter or cream.

Broiling

Next to a grill, the broiler is a girl's best friend for fast cooking. In fact, broiling is an urban girl's low-tech upside-down grill, great for flavorful, thin cuts, such as steaks, chops, and cutlets, as well as kebabs. The direct heat of broiling browns and caramelizes the meat's surface, creating a flavorful crust.

Basic Broiling: Preheat the broiler for at least 5 minutes. Line the tray part of the broiler pan with aluminum foil for easy cleanup. Adjust the distance of the rack from the heat according to the thickness of the meat, usually 3 to 4 inches for a 1- to 2-inch-thick cut, 5 to 8 inches for a 3-inch or thicker cut, and 1 to 2 inches for extra-thin cutlets that are less than 1 inch thick.

Brush the meat with oil, season with salt and pepper, and place on the lined broiler pan. Broil for about 10 minutes per inch of thickness. Cutlets are so thin that they don't usually even need to be flipped. For thicker cuts, turn halfway through the cooking time. For the thickest cuts, start the meat a good distance from the broiler element, and then brown the meat by moving the rack up to finish.

Grilling

This is the cooking method for girls who like to play with fire! Grilling sears the meat and imparts a distinctive smoky flavor that can vary depending on whether you use charcoal or gas. Burgers are probably the most common grilling fare, but everything from thick, flat steaks, cutlets, ribs, and kebabs to a leg of lamb and a tri-tip are possible. Always trim away extra fat to prevent drippings that can cause flare-ups, and be sure the meat is at room temperature before it hits the fire.

Basic Grilling: Light the grill. If you are using charcoal, let it burn down until it is covered with a light coating of gray ash (20 to 25 minutes), then spread it evenly over the bottom. (If using a gas grill, let preheat for 15 minutes and you'll be ready to go.) Lightly oil the cooking grate and set it over the fire. The grill is ready when the grate is hot and you can comfortably hold your hand about 6 inches above the fire for no more than 3 or 4 seconds. Brush the meat with oil, season with salt and pepper, and place on the grill directly over the fire (this is known as direct grilling). Grill, turning once halfway through the estimated cooking time, until cooked to desired doneness.

For larger cuts such as roasts, grill meat next to, not over, the fire. Light the fire as directed, and when the charcoal is covered with ash, push it to one side and place a drip pan on the other side. If using a gas grill, turn on all the burners to preheat, and then turn off the burner(s) on one side of the grill. Place the meat on the cooking grate over the drip pan (not over the coals) or turned-off burner(s), close the lid, and open the vents. (This is known as indirect grilling.) The effect is similar to oven roasting, with cooking times about the same.

Pan Roasting

Fast and easy, pan roasting is two methods in one for one-pan cooking at its best. First, you brown the meat on the stove top in a skillet to seal in the flavor and second, you roast the meat in the same pan in the oven to the desired doneness. With only one pan, you have less mess, plus by shifting the meat to the oven, you free up the stove top to cook other things, which is always handy for girls who like to multi-task. Just make sure to use an ovenproof skillet. Pan roasting is the ideal method for thicker steaks and chops—porterhouse or rib-eye steaks, double lamb chops, or center-cut pork chops—in part because it cuts down on smoky kitchens.

Basic Pan Roasting: Preheat the oven to 350°F. Pat the meat dry and season it with salt and pepper. Heat an ovenproof skillet over high heat. Add a little oil or some butter and heat until nearly smoking. Add the meat and sear well on both sides, but no more than about 1 minute per side. Slip the pan into the oven and cook the meat to desired doneness.

Roasting

Whether you are roasting a leg of lamb for six or a pork tenderloin for two, your house will fill with phenomenal aromas. This simple dry-heat method enhances the meat's natural flavors. You can roast with or without a rack in the pan, but we recommend using one for more even cooking. You can slip a few potatoes or other vegetables along-side your roast so that your side dishes are ready when your meat is. The best cuts to roast? The classics, of course: standing rib, boneless pork loin, shoulder, and leg of lamb.

Basic Roasting: Trim the meat of excess fat, place on a rack in a shallow roasting pan just large enough to accommodate it, and bring to room temperature. Meanwhile, preheat the oven to 450°F. Lightly coat the meat with oil, season generously with salt and pepper, and roast until browned. Lower the heat to 350°F and roast to desired doneness. Let the meat rest before carving.

Sautéing

We Meat Club girls are always busy, so fast, easy sautéing is an indispensable technique in our cooking repertoire. A pan, a stove top, and oil and you're ready to go. The added benefits are the pan juices that can be easily transformed into simple sauces on their own or by deglazing the pan with wine or some other delicious liquid. The best cuts for sautéing include thin, flat steaks, chops and cut-lets, ground-meat patties, and sausages. Thicker versions of these same cuts are better suited to pan roasting.

Basic Sautéing: Preheat a skillet over high heat. Pat the meat dry and season with salt and pepper. Add a little oil, clarified butter, or butter and oil and heat until nearly smoking. Add the meat in a sin-gle layer, making sure not to crowd the pieces (too crowded and they'll steam and turn gray, rather than become a gorgeous chestnut brown). Cook, turning once or occasionally, depending on the recipe, until the meat is well browned and cooked to desired doneness. To make a simple sauce, deglaze the pan with stock, wine, or any other flavorful cooking liquid, stirring to dislodge the tasty, brown bits from the pan bottom. Strain the sauce, if desired, before serving.

Stewing

In the Meat Club, we like to make slow-cooked stews for cozy meals. Like braising, the meat is simmered in liquid, but, as we pointed out earlier, the differences are the amount of liquid—here the meat is fully covered, not just halfway—and often the smaller size of the pieces. Submerging the meat in liquid helps to tenderize it, while the meat more fully absorbs the flavor of the liquid. The key to a good stew is patience. Shanks, top round, chuck, and cubed beef and lamb are just a few of the candidates for your stew pot.

Basic Stewing: The initial steps for stewing are the same as for braising. You pat the meat dry, season, dust with flour, and brown well on all sides. Once the meat is browned, add enough liquid (stock, wine, or beer, or a combination) to cover the meat completely. Bring to a simmer, cover, and cook on the stove top or in a moderate oven (350°F) until a knife slides easily into the meat. This can take as little as an hour or as long as 3 hours. Lift out the meat with a slotted spoon and cook the liquid rapidly on the stove top until thickened enough to coat the back of a spoon lightly, then serve the meat in the reduced liquid.

Essential Meat Club Cooking Equipment

Every meat girl needs a few basic tools. You can buy all kinds of equipment for your meat cooking adventures, but to start, you just need a few essential items...

BROILER PAN: Buy the biggest pan that will fit under your broiler.

CARVING/CUTTING BOARDS: It's good to have more than one! For carving, a large wooden board with an outside groove to catch all the juices is essential.

ENAMELED CAST-IRON CASSEROLE OR DUTCH OVEN: A heavy casserole or Dutch oven will make your roasts, braises, and stews come out beautifully and will last you a very long time.

KNIVES: A set of high-quality knives is far and away the most important meat tool you can have. Though we leave the fancy cutting (butterflying and frenching) to the butcher, we like to have a full set of knives for paring, carving, and chopping. We prefer high-carbon stainless steel for our knives. Always hand-wash your knives and have them sharpened once a year by your butcher.

MEAT MALLET: A meat mallet is an invaluable tool for pounding and tenderizing filets and cutlets.

MEAT THERMOMETER: A meat-thermometer is the best investment you can make. We use old-fashioned dial thermometers in the style of our mothers, but a modern digital instant-read will guarantee good meat cooking every time.

ROASTING PANS: A good roasting pan with a nonstick rack is necessary for (you guessed it!) roasting. Buy the biggest one that will fit into your oven.

SAUTÉ PANS: For sautéing and pan frying, you'll need a set of sauté pans or skillets with ovenproof handles. We recommend having large and small pans in both stainless steel and cast iron.

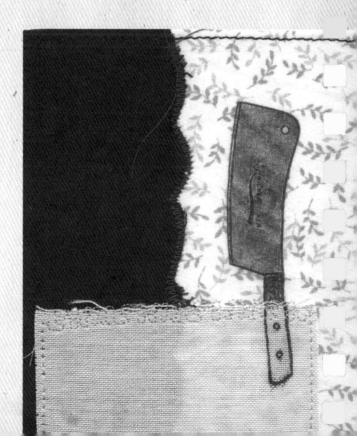

Chapter Two
Beef It Up!

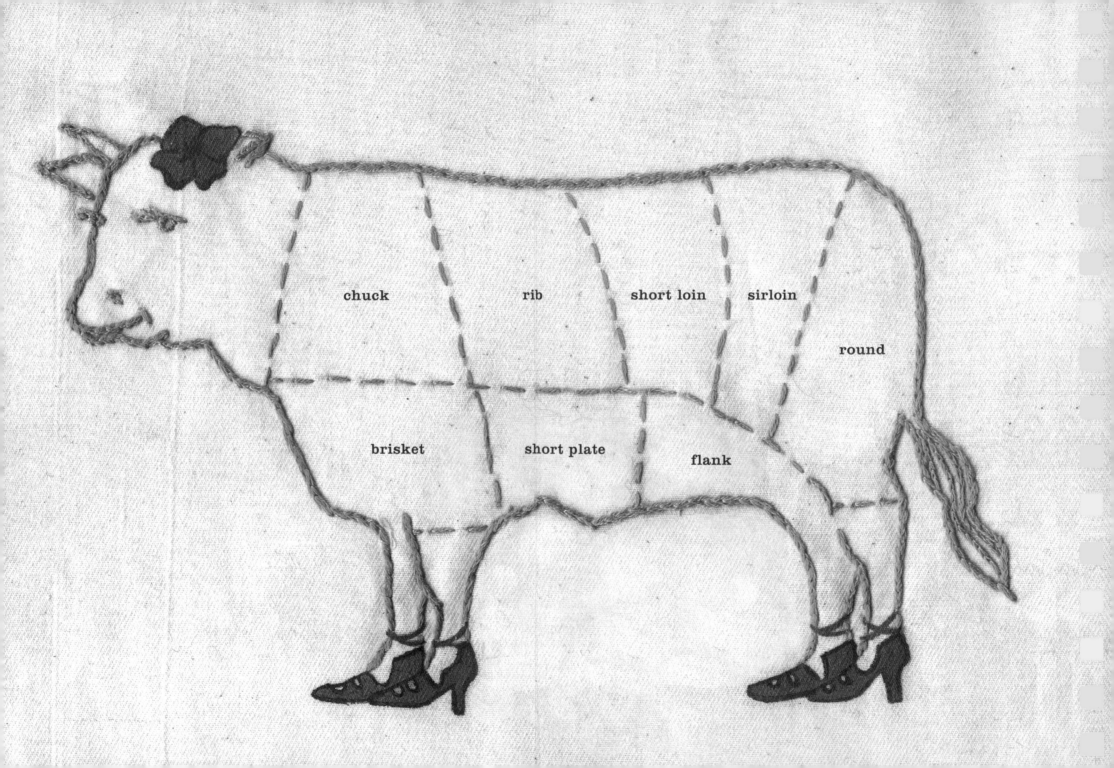

A London broil was at the center of one of our first, most memorable, and most disastrous Meat Club nights. We made the mistake of trying to broil the steak in a Pyrex pan that promptly blew up. No one was hurt (except for the steak) but we learned our lesson. Since that time we've made it our business to know the beef about beef.

By far the most popular of all, beef is really the king (or empress) of meats. Cut from the cow, beef is big in size and flavor. (When you compare something to a side of beef, you are talking big!) With so many cuts from which to choose—from the classic American burger to fancy roasts to the ultimate and infinite possibilities of steak—it's no wonder that beef is the most popular meat, especially in America, where the average American eats sixty-three pounds of beef a year!

Beef is rich in protein and such nutrients as iron, zinc, folic acid, and other B vitamins—all of them essential to keeping girls healthy. We highly recommend natural beef raised on land that is cared for, without growth-promoting hormones.

We all grew up eating more beef than any other meat and many of the recipes in this section are updates of classic recipes from our mothers and grandmothers. We've shared many a child-hood memory over pot roasts, homemade spaghetti and meatballs, and meat loaves. To this collection, we've also added a few culinary surprises, including flat-iron steak with an onion relish (page 40) and a spirited tequila-infused tri-tip (page 51), as well as more exotic favorites including Korean short ribs (page 70) and a tasty beef satay (page 58).

In this chapter we've tried to pare it down to the essentials with basic information for buying and choosing good beef, a basic guide to the cuts we love, and a variety of recipes for a beautiful beef-eating experience.

The Meaty Basics: Beef

Making the Grade

Beef is sold under eight grades, defined primarily by flavor and tenderness—qualities that hinge largely on how much marbling (internal fat) the meat has. Despite this bounty of classifications, most consumers see only the top of the heap: Prime, Choice, and Select. Prime is the best and most fatty, but most Prime beef ends up in the kitchens of top-end steakhouses or is shipped abroad for big bucks. It is pretty tender and tasty, so if you find it, buy it. Choice is the next grade down and is, along with Select, what most retail butchers sell. Your best bet is to ask your butcher to help you find the finest Choice meat in the counter. Also, beware of fantasy names that sound like grades—Butcher's Prime, Market Choice—but aren't.

You've Got the Look

Beef should be firm, fine textured, and a nice bright cherry red (try to get a peek in natural light, if possible). The exception is dry-aged beef, which is darker in color. Pass up any cut with soft-looking red bones; yellow, rather than creamy white, fat; or two-toned or deep red flesh. Most beef should show off its marbling without looking too fatty, smell fresh, and never be sticky or dripping wet.

Favorite Flavorings

From a simple rub of salt and pepper to marinades to fancy cream sauces, beef pairs with a wide range of flavors. Our favorite seasonings to put in marinades and sauces include pungent herbs such as rosemary, oregano, garlic, garlic, and garlic. Did we mention garlic? Rich cheese, such as Gorgonzola, Maytag blue, and Roquefort, also complements the hefty flavors of a tasty piece of beef.

Cook It Right

As a general rule, the tender cuts such as sirloin, tenderloin, and rib-eye are best simply grilled or roasted, and cooked rare. The tougher cuts—like chuck, round, and brisket—are best when braised or stewed, to break down the collagen and absorb the flavor of the cooking liquid. Below are general internal temperatures for beef.

RARE: 120°–130°F

MEDIUM-RARE: 130°–135°F

MEDIUM: 140°–150°F

MEDIUM-WELL: 155°–165°F

WELL DONE: 170°–185°F

As for the tougher cuts, it isn't necessarily the temperature that indicates when it is done but rather when the meat is tender to the fork.

Storing Beef

Store steaks and other packaged cuts in the coldest part of the refrigerator (usually the bottom) for up to four days; a two-day maximum for ground beef. Well-wrapped frozen beef will last from three to six months.

The Mystique of the Cow Physique

The cow is divided into eight primal cuts (see figure on fold-out): chuck, rib, short loin, sirloin, round, flank, short plate, and brisket.

CHUCK: This is found behind the neck/shoulder area of the cow, back to the fifth rib. The meat can be intensely flavorful and relatively tough but is especially good ground for burgers and meatballs. Steaks from the chuck are also quite flavorful, especially flat-iron steaks and top blade steaks, though not as tender as those from the rib, short loin, or sirloin. Meat from the chuck is especially good for stews, braises, and pot roasts. Great cuts for roasting include the chuck-eye roast, the under blade pot roast, and the flavorful chuck rib roast—a terrific cut for pot roast such as our Hankee Pankee Yankee Pot Roast (page 64).

RIB: One of the most delicious and valuable cuts, the rib is as good as it gets. The meat is very tasty and is generally sold as steaks and roasts. The standing rib roast (also known as the prime rib roast) is classic party (holiday) fare. We also love back ribs braised in liquid, but our all-time favorite has to be the rib-eye roast, which we love to slather with herbs and spices like in our flavorful recipe for Garlic-Infused Rib-Eye Roast (page 63).

SHORT LOIN: You've got to love your loins because these are the most tasty and tender cuts. Found directly behind the rib, the loin or short loin is known for its tender and delicious steaks and roasts. Meat from the loin is often sold at a premium price, but worth it for those special occasions and special people in our lives. Our favorite loin steaks include the New York strip (also known as a shell steak, club steak, or strip loin steak), tenderloin (also known as filet mignon), T-bone, and porterhouse. For roasts, we are particularly fond of the top loin as well as the tenderloin roasts.

SIRLOIN: Both flavorful and tender, the sirloin is found behind the loin and the flank. We love cuts such as the tri-tip, sirloin, and top sirloin steaks, including round bone, pin bone, and other steaks with names too numerous to list here. We also love to use ground sirloin for tender, tasty burgers.

ROUND: A round rear is fully appreciated on a cow and is best used as ground meat. Though the round is often cut into steaks such as the top round (or rump steak) and roasts (top or bottom round), these cuts are very flavorful and they are great for making pot roasts. When spiced and infused with seasoning, ground round is great for meat-balls and meatloaf.

FLANK and **SHORT PLATE:** If you like your meat lean and tasty, the flank is for you. Most often cut into steaks, the flank is found directly under the loin. Steaks cut from the flank include the London broil and other steaks that are labeled either skirt steak or flank steak. They are delicious when marinated and grilled. Located next to the flank, the plate includes the very flavorful hanger steak, but typically plate meat is tough and best used in a stew.

BRISKET: Brisket is one of the toughest of cuts, but with a little love and a lot of time, a good braise will transform this cut into a wonder-fully comforting dish as with our Slow-Lovin' Beef Brisket (page 66). The brisket, found right under the chuck, is often used commercially to make corned beef and pastrami.

We encourage you to get to know your beef cut by cut and whenever possible, Beef It Up!

What's at Steak?

★ ★ ★

When it comes right down to it, nothing feeds a beef craving better than a juicy steak. Steak nights at the Meat Club are always happy nights. Over the years we've sampled our share of sumptuous steaks and we each have a favorite: Gemma loves the buttery texture of a tender filet mignon, especially topped with a rich Gorgonzola sauce; Kristina desires the deep flavor of a porterhouse; and Vanessa prefers the chewy pleasure of a flat-iron steak. A steak's flavor and texture will vary greatly depending on its cut. Each kind of steak has its particular delicious qualities; what you prefer will depend on what matters most to you.

Broadly speaking, steaks from the loin and the rib are the most tender and are best grilled or pan grilled. Steaks from the sirloin and round are deliciously flavored and more reasonably priced. Those from the flank and chuck usually have excellent flavor but vary widely in tenderness. For every steak there is a seasoning, and for every mood there is a marinade. Sauces, rubs, and marinades add flavor and will enhance and even tenderize certain cuts.

With so many steak choices it can be difficult to know what to ask for. To make matters more confusing, many steaks have names that vary by region and even in which market they are sold. Below are some general steak guidelines to help get you started. When having doubts, consult your friend and ours, the butcher.

Short Loin Steaks: If you value tenderness, loin steaks are for you. Short loin steaks are the most tender and are so delicious. They are not generally as flavorful as some of the other cuts and are thus especially good marinated or sauced for extra flavor.

Name Games: T-bones; porterhouse; tenderloin steaks (also known as filet mignon, *filet de boeuf,* filet); top loin steaks; boneless (also known as Ambassador, strip, boneless club, hotel-style, Kansas City, New York strips, veiny); and bone-in top loin steaks (also known as chip club, club, country club, Delmonico, shell, sirloin strip, strip).

Cook It Up: Grill, sauté, broil, or pan broil all short loin steaks.

A Seasoning to Remember: A simple salting may do the trick, but loin steaks are especially good sauced.

Rib Steaks: Though not quite as tender as steaks from the short loin, rib steaks are next in line and are often tastier than loin steaks. We love both bone-in rib steaks as well as boneless rib-eye steaks.

Name Games: Rib steaks are also called market, Spencer, Delmonico, beauty, and entrecôte.

Cook It Up: Grill, sauté, broil, or pan broil all rib steaks.

A Seasoning to Remember: Great with rubs and marinades.

Hanger, Flank, and Skirt Steaks: What these steaks lack in tenderness, they make up for in deep beefy flavor. These steaks are improved ten-fold when marinated overnight.

Name Games: Hanger steak (also known as hanging tenderloin, butcher's, hanging tender); flank steak (also know as flank steak filet, jiffy, London broil—London broil was once exclusively from the flank but now it means any lean, less-expensive steak from the top round, sirloin, or even the shoulder); and skirt steak (also known as Philadelphia, fajita meat, inside skirt, outside skirt).

Cook It Up: Grill, broil, pan broil, or (with the exception of the flank steak) sauté.

A Seasoning to Remember: Best marinated overnight.

Sirloin Steaks: Whether your pocketbook is real or faux Chanel, sirloin steaks give great bang for the buck. Sirloin steaks are very tasty and very popular, especially with a marinade or dry rub, and are much leaner than New York or rib-eye steaks.

Name Games: Sirloin steaks (also known as flat bone, pin bone, round bone, wedge bone); top sirloin steak; boneless (also known as sirloin butt, London broil); and tri-tip steak (also known as culotte or triangle).

Cook It Up: Grill, broil, pan broil, or sauté.

A Seasoning to Remember: Best prepared with a dry rub.

Round Steaks: Relatively lean, these steaks are delicious and kind to the figure but certain cuts can be a bit chewy. Round steaks include the bottom round steak, the London broil steak, and the round tip steak.

Name Games: Round tip steak (also known as ball tip, beef sirloin tip, breakfast, knuckle, sandwich, minute); round steak (also known as full-cut round); top round steak (also known as top round London broil); and eye round steak (which, when cooked, is known as Swiss steak).

Cook It up: Top round steaks are very lean and should be marinated overnight and cooked quickly. Both the bottom round and round steaks are best braised.

A Seasoning to Remember: Both the round tip and top round steaks are best marinated.

Chuck Steaks: Home of one of our favorites, the flat-iron steak, chuck steaks are known for their intense flavor. They can be quite tender, as is the case with chuck shoulder and rib-bone chuck—but many steaks from this cut can be a bit chewy and have a line of gristle. Remove it with a knife. We recommend marinating these steaks overnight.

Name Games: top blade steak; boneless (also known as flat-iron, book, butler, lifter, petite, top chuck, blade); boneless shoulder steak (also known as clod, English, London broil, shoulder steak half cut); chuck arm steak (also known as arm Swiss, chuck for Swissing, round bone); boneless chuck-eye steak (also known as boneless chuck filet, boneless bottom chuck, boneless chuck slices); chuck mock tender steak (also known as chuck-eye, chuck filet, fish, chuck tender); and chuck 7-bone steak (also known as the center-chuck).

Cook It Up: Grill, broil, pan broil, or braise top blade steaks (boneless), shoulder steaks (boneless), and chuck-eye steaks (boneless). Chuck arm steaks and chuck 7-bone steaks are best braised.

A Seasoning to Remember: Marinate top blade, boneless shoulder, and chuck-eye steaks (boneless).

London Broil—What the Heck Is It?

As you've probably noticed by now, London broil is listed in many of the sections above. Let's set the record straight, girls. The term London broil actually refers to a cooking method, not one specific cut of beef. The recipe first appeared in print in the 1930s and consisted of a flank steak, which was broiled and sliced thinly across the grain. Hanger, skirt, top round, and chuck steaks can also be prepared this way, which is why you'll find the term used loosely in the meat world.

Sauces and Marinades

★ ★ ★

The Meat Club loves their steaks naked, but here are some
sure-fire ways to dress them up when necessary.

Sweet 'n' Easy Marinade
MAKES 3/4 CUP

1/2 cup honey

1/4 cup soy sauce

3 tablespoons olive oil

4 garlic cloves, crushed

1 stem fresh rosemary

Whisk together all the ingredients, pour over the meat,
and marinate for at least 2 hours in the refrigerator.

Meat Club Rub
MAKES ENOUGH TO COVER FOUR 1/2-POUND STEAKS

2 tablespoons ground coriander

2 tablespoons ground coffee

1 tablespoon salt

1 tablespoon freshly ground black pepper

1 teaspoon ground chipotle pepper

Mix all the ingredients thoroughly in a self-sealing plastic bag.
Generously coat the meat on all sides.

Hunky Chunky Relish
MAKES 5 CUPS

1/4 cup balsamic vinegar

4 teaspoons chopped fresh oregano

3/4 cup olive oil

1/4 cup drained canned diced mild green chiles

4 scallions, finely chopped

4 cups halved cherry tomatoes

Salt

Freshly ground black pepper

Whisk the vinegar and oregano in a medium bowl to blend. Gradually whisk in the oil. Mix in the chiles and scallions. Cover and refrigerate for 2 hours. Toss in the tomatoes when ready to serve. Season with salt and pepper.

Roquefort Butter
MAKES 1/2 CUP

1 shallot, finely diced

1 teaspoon olive oil

1/2 cup (4 ounces) Roquefort cheese

4 tablespoons (1/2 stick) unsalted butter, softened

1 tablespoon chopped fresh flat-leaf parsley

In a small pan, lightly sauté the shallot in the oil over medium heat until translucent. Let cool to room temperature.

In a bowl, combine the shallot, cheese, butter, and parsley with a fork. Mix until blended. Spread on grilled steaks or hamburgers.

Green Goddess Sauce
MAKES 1 CUP

1 garlic clove, minced

1/2 teaspoon salt

1 cup fresh cilantro, chopped

1/4 cup olive oil

2 tablespoons fresh lemon juice

1/8 teaspoon cayenne pepper

Put the garlic and salt into a small bowl and mash into a paste. Transfer the paste to a mini food processor. Add the remaining ingredients and blend well.

Peppy Horseradish Sauce
MAKES 1 CUP

2 ciabatta rolls, crusts removed and cut into 1-inch cubes

3 tablespoons olive oil

1/4 cup prepared horseradish

1 garlic clove, crushed

Salt

Freshly ground black pepper

Mix all the ingredients in a mini food processor until well blended.

Dreamy, Creamy Ancho Sauce
MAKES ¼ CUP

1 teaspoon butter

1 small shallot, chopped

1 small ancho chile, diced

¼ teaspoon cumin seeds

¼ teaspoon finely chopped fresh oregano

⅔ cup light cream

Salt

Freshly ground black pepper

Melt the butter in a small saucepan over medium heat. Add the shallot, chile, cumin, and oregano and sauté until the shallot is translucent, about 10 minutes. Pour in the cream and simmer, until the sauce thickens, stirring occasionally, about 20 minutes. Add salt and pepper to taste.

Sweet Zinger Pepper Sauce
MAKES 2 CUPS

One 12-ounce jar roasted red peppers

1 cup fresh basil

¼ cup cream

2 anchovy fillets

Salt

Freshly ground black pepper

Mix all the ingredients in a mini food processor until well blended.

Flat-Iron Steak with Warm Onion Relish

The Meat Club loves a good steak. Cut from the chuck and rich with flavor, flat-iron steaks are wonderful simply seasoned with salt and pepper and grilled or pan seared, as they are here. A popular favorite at restaurants, flat-iron steaks are also known as top blade chuck steaks and book steaks, among other names. Vanessa tried this cut as recommended by an artisan butcher at Potter Farms in the San Francisco Ferry Plaza Farmers Market. Of course, you can use this recipe for other flavorful steaks such as sirloins, T-bones, or porterhouses.

SERVES 4

Warm Onion Relish

2 tablespoons olive oil

1 bunch large spring onions, white parts only, thinly sliced

3 garlic cloves, thinly sliced

2 tablespoons balsamic vinegar

2 tablespoons red wine

1 tablespoon packed brown sugar

1 tablespoon olive oil

Four 1½-inch-thick flat-iron steaks (6 to 8 ounces each)

Salt

Freshly ground black pepper

1. To make the Onion Relish: In a large skillet or sauté pan, add the oil, onions, and garlic and cook over medium heat, stirring occasionally, until tender, about 6 minutes. Add more oil if the garlic and onions begin to stick to the pan.

2. Add the vinegar, wine, and brown sugar and bring to a simmer. Cook over medium heat for 5 minutes, or until the liquid is reduced. Makes about ½ cup. (Extra relish will keep, covered in the refrigerator, for up to 3 days. Reheat over low heat until warm.)

3. To make the steaks: In a large, deep skillet, heat the oil until hot. Generously season the meat with salt and pepper, add to the skillet, and cook over medium-high heat for about 3 minutes on each side for medium-rare.

4. Let the steaks rest, covered loosely with foil, for 5 minutes before serving with the Warm Onion Relish.

Busty Burgers

When it comes to the ultimate beef-eating experience, we'd say it was a toss-up between a juicy steak and the classic American burger. For our ladies' burger nights, we set up a burger bar with all the fixings: grilled onions, dill pickles, avocados, fresh basil, horseradish, spicy relishes, and bacon, as well as the regular ketchup and mayonnaise. To give a little added surprise to the classic burger, we stuff our burgers with a soft cheese such as Gorgonzola, fresh goat, or Maytag blue. We prefer using ground sirloin meat, which is 20% fat—ground chuck is more fatty (between 20% and 25% fat), while ground round can be too lean (between 10% and 15% fat).

SERVES 4

2 pounds lean ground beef, preferably ground sirloin

1 teaspoon salt

1/2 teaspoon freshly ground black pepper

1 cup (8 ounces) Gorgonzola or blue cheese

1 tablespoon butter, softened

2 tablespoons olive oil

1. In a large bowl, combine the meat, salt, and pepper. Form into 4 evenly shaped patties. Refrigerate while you make the stuffing.

2. Put the cheese in a bowl and blend in the butter thoroughly with a fork until creamy.

3. Remove the patties from the fridge and place equal amounts of the stuffing in the center of each patty. Reshape the patties to make sure the stuffing is encircled (enveloped) with meat mixture.

4. Heat the oil in a skillet or sauté pan over medium-high. Sauté the burgers for 4 minutes per side for medium-rare. Enjoy with all your favorite fixings.

Old School Chili

This recipe is a family favorite, passed on by Kristina's aunt. The chili is flavorful but not too spicy, so even Kristina's daughter, Lucy, a bean fanatic, enjoys eating it. The Meat Club prefers to use ground chuck for this one. It has a higher fat content and tastes more flavorful than other cuts. Crackers make a great accompaniment (we like good ol' standard saltines) as well as warm flour or corn tortillas. Serve up a crisp green salad with slices of orange and jicama to round out the meal.

SERVES 4 TO 6

3 tablespoons olive oil

1 pound ground chuck

One 28-ounce can chopped tomatoes

2 medium onions, coarsely chopped

1 green bell pepper, diced

3 tablespoons chili powder

1 teaspoon cayenne pepper

2 garlic cloves, minced

Two 15-ounce cans red kidney beans

Salt

Freshly ground black pepper

1. Heat the oil in a large saucepan over medium heat until hot. Add the beef and brown while stirring, about 5 minutes.

2. Add the tomatoes, onions, bell pepper, chili powder, cayenne, and garlic. Cover and simmer for about 1 hour, stirring frequently to prevent sticking.

3. Add the beans and simmer another 20 minutes, until the beans are heated through. Taste and add salt and pepper as needed.

Spaghetti Beers Bolognese

The Beers Bolognese was first given to Kristina's aunt when she began dating her future husband, Bob Beers. Little did she know it would grow into a family favorite for generations to come. Although there are many versions of this classic Italian meat sauce, named after the region from which it originated, all Bolognese sauces have one thing in common: The longer it cooks, the better it gets. This version combines the flavors of beef and pork for those of us who agree that ONE meat just isn't enough!

SERVES 4 TO 6

3 tablespoons olive oil

1 pound ground beef

8 ounces ground pork

One 28-ounce can whole tomatoes, with their juices

Two 6-ounce cans tomato paste

1 large onion, chopped

1 green bell pepper, chopped

3 tablespoons chopped fresh basil

3 garlic cloves, minced

1 bay leaf

Salt

Freshly ground black pepper

1 pound spaghetti or other pasta

1. Heat the oil in a large sauté pan or skillet. Add the beef and pork and cook until brown, while stirring, about 5 minutes.

2. Stir in the tomatoes and juice, tomato paste, onion, bell pepper, basil, garlic, and bay leaf. Cover and simmer 1½ hours, stirring frequently, to blend the flavors.

3. Remove the bay leaf and set aside. Taste the sauce and add salt and pepper as needed.

4. Boil 6 quarts water and 2 tablespoons salt in a large pot.

5. When water has come to a rapid boil, add the spaghetti and stir for 30 seconds so the pasta does not stick together.

6. Boil for 8 to 10 minutes (we like it a little al dente) and drain.

7. Divide the pasta among plates, and serve with the sauce.

Grams' Italian Meatballs with Spaghetti

Whenever Gemma and her five brothers and sisters visited their grandmother (whom everyone called Grams), she would have a big batch of meatballs ready for everyone! Grams eventually taught Gemma how to make this treasured recipe, so now at all the Meat Club family gatherings, Gemma is the one who brings a fresh batch to the party! We like to serve our meatballs over spaghetti (in the classic style we remember from our childhoods) but these meatballs are good served over any pasta or unadorned as an appetizer.

Make sure that you do not make the meatballs too large or they may fall apart when browning. Meatballs and sauce may be made two days ahead. Reheat meatballs in sauce before serving.

**MAKES 45 MEATBALLS;
SERVES 8 TO 10**

Meatballs

1 cup plain dried bread crumbs

1¼ cups milk

1 onion, finely chopped

½ cup (4 ounces) grated Parmesan cheese

⅓ cup fresh flat-leaf parsley, minced

2 large eggs

2 tablespoons minced garlic

1. To make the meatballs: In a large bowl, soak the bread crumbs in the milk for 10 minutes, or until the milk is absorbed.

2. Add the onion, ½ cup cheese, parsley, eggs, garlic, salt, and pepper to the bread and milk and lightly mix together. Add the beef, veal, and pork to the mixture and continue to gently mix with your hands; be sure not to overmix.

3. Roll the mixture between your hands to form into 1½-inch balls and arrange on large trays or baking sheets.

4. In a heavy sauté pan with deep sides, heat the oil over medium heat and brown the meatballs in batches without crowding. The meatballs should be brown on all sides but will not be cooked through. They will finish cooking when simmering in the sauce.

1 tablespoon salt

³/₄ teaspoon freshly
ground black pepper

2 pounds ground beef

8 ounces ground veal

8 ounces ground pork

¹/₂ cup olive oil

Tomato Sauce

Two 32-ounce cans
whole plum tomatoes

1 tablespoon minced garlic

1 teaspoon dried oregano

2 tablespoons minced
fresh flat-leaf parsley

Salt

Freshly ground black pepper

1 pound spaghetti
or other pasta

Grated Parmesan
cheese for sprinkling

5. Remove the meatballs from the pan and place on a large plate.

6. To make the Tomato Sauce: Strain the tomatoes, reserving the juice, and chop the tomatoes or crush with your hands. In the same pan in which you cooked the meatballs, add the tomatoes and the reserved juices, the garlic, and the oregano. Simmer for 30 minutes. (Using the same pan with all of the oil and bits of meat will add to the flavor of the sauce.)

7. Add the meatballs to the sauce and continue to simmer about 20 minutes, until the meatballs are cooked through.

8. Add the parsley and season with salt and pepper. Remove from the heat.

9. Boil 6 quarts water and 1 tablespoon salt in a large pot.

10. When water has come to a rapid boil, add the spaghetti and stir for 30 seconds so the pasta does not stick together.

11. Boil the pasta for 8 to 10 minutes (we like it a little al dente) and drain.

12. Place the pasta in a large serving bowl and add the meatballs and sauce on top.

13. Sprinkle with Parmesan cheese and serve immediately.

Mini Meat Pies

This Meat Club recipe made it to Vanessa's date night. Vanessa and her beau had a weekly ritual of tuning into *The Sopranos* on Sunday nights and these individual pies were the perfect dinner for two. A complete meal-in-one, these are hearty and extremely versatile. Serve with a bottle of your favorite red. If you prefer, you can substitute ground lamb for the ground beef. Whichever you choose, make sure it's on the lean side. The Meat Club loves using Niman Ranch ground beef. You'll need two 14-ounce ramekins or ovenproof bowls.

SERVES 2

6 medium yellow potatoes, preferably Yukon golds, diced

3 carrots, diced

1 rib celery, diced

1/2 cup frozen peas with pearl onions

1 tablespoon fresh marjoram leaves, plus a few whole sprigs to decorate crust

1 tablespoon olive oil

1 onion, chopped

1 garlic clove, crushed

1 1/2 pounds ground beef

1 teaspoon dried basil

1. Preheat the oven to 350°F.

2. Put the potatoes, carrots, and celery in a medium saucepan and cover with water. Bring to a boil and simmer for about 10 minutes, or until soft.

3. Drain and return to the saucepan. Stir in the peas and onions and 1 tablespoon marjoram. Remove from the heat and set aside.

4. Heat the oil in a large sauté pan or skillet over medium heat. Add the onion and garlic and sauté for 5 minutes, until softened. Add the beef, basil, and oregano. Stir and cook until browned, about 10 minutes.

5. Add the broth and wine. Simmer for 5 minutes longer to incorporate the liquids, remove from the heat, and set aside. Season with the salt and pepper.

6. Unwrap the pastry dough and lay flat. Place two 14-ounce ramekins on top of the dough and cut around them, leaving 1/8 inch extra around each for tucking the dough into the edges.

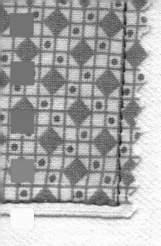

1 teaspoon dried oregano

¼ cup beef broth

2 tablespoons red wine

1 teaspoon salt

1 teaspoon freshly
ground black pepper

1 sheet frozen flaky
pastry dough, thawed for
2 hours at room temperature

7. Spoon half of the beef mixture in one of the ramekins and top with half of the vegetable mixture. Repeat with the second ramekin.

8. Place the pastry rounds on top of each and tuck in the edges. Place a sprig or two of fresh marjoram in the center of each. Bake for 30 to 35 minutes, or until the dough is golden. Let rest for 5 minutes before cutting into these.

Stuff It with Bacon Meatloaf

Two of our Italian grandmothers had something in common: They both made meatloaf topped with strips of bacon! The Meat Club felt that the bacon was definitely the best part of the dish, so we decided to "stuff" our version instead! The bacon permeates the loaf with a rich smoky flavor. We recommend letting the meatloaf "marinate" overnight, but you can bake it right away if you can't wait.

SERVES 6

Butter or oil for greasing

1 egg

1 cup milk

3 cups soft white fresh bread crumbs

1 pound bacon

2 pounds lean ground beef

1 onion, finely chopped

1/2 cup chopped celery

1/4 cup chopped fresh parsley

3 tablespoons ketchup, plus extra for serving

1. Preheat the oven to 350°F.

2. Grease a 9-by-5-inch loaf pan.

3. Beat the egg and milk together in a large bowl. Add the bread crumbs and mix gently. Let the mixture stand for 15 minutes, or until the bread absorbs the milk.

4. Meanwhile, in a large sauté pan, brown 14 slices of the bacon until crisp. Remove the strips and drain on paper towels. Chop into 1/2-inch pieces.

5. Add the beef, onion, celery, parsley, ketchup, 2 tablespoons hot sauce (if using), salt, pepper, basil, thyme, and browned bacon to the bread-crumb mixture. Roll up your sleeves and mix well with your hands. (Don't be afraid of getting dirty!) Refrigerate overnight if possible.

6. Pat the mixture into the prepared pan in an even layer.

2 tablespoons hot sauce
(optional), plus extra for serving

1¾ teaspoons salt

1½ teaspoons freshly
ground black pepper

¼ teaspoon dried basil

¼ teaspoon dried thyme

7. Top the loaf with the remaining slices of raw bacon. Bake for 55 minutes, or until the meat is firm to the touch and has shrunk from the sides of the pan. Let rest for 15 minutes before slicing. Serve with plenty of extra ketchup and hot sauce.

Royal Broil with Balsamic Bliss

Although the name London broil is now given to any inexpensive, lean, tender steak from the top round, sirloin, or even the shoulder, London broil was originally the name of a steak from the flank that was marinated, grilled, and cut across the grain. The Meat Club discovered the secret to a tender broil is to marinate it for at least three hours.

SERVES 4

2 pounds London broil, preferably from the flank

¼ cup packed brown sugar

2 tablespoons balsamic vinegar

2 tablespoons freshly ground black pepper

¼ cup red wine

1 tablespoon Chinese hot chili sauce

1. Place the meat in a heavy-duty self-sealing plastic bag with the brown sugar, vinegar, and pepper. Marinate for at least 3 hours in the refrigerator.

2. Preheat the broiler or a grill to high heat.

3. Remove the meat from the bag, reserving the marinade, place on a broiler pan or the grill over direct heat, and cook for about 5 minutes per side for medium-rare. Transfer the meat to a cutting board and cover loosely with foil; let stand for 5 minutes.

4. Add the reserved marinade to a small skillet with the wine and chili sauce. Bring to a boil, reduce the heat, and simmer, for 5 to 10 minutes, or until the sauce is reduced by half. Thinly slice the meat against the grain and serve with the Balsamic Bliss.

Marinated Tri-Tipsy

Vanessa once seduced a vegetarian into eating meat with this spirited recipe for tri-tip. Tri-tip roasts, cut from the bottom part of the sirloin, are also sometimes called triangle roasts and are excellent cooked at high temperatures. Tri-tips are also wonderful massaged with dry rubs or marinated, and with this lime-infused tequila concoction you are sure to have lively dinner conversations. The two hours of marinating will give you plenty of time to enjoy a margarita or two.

SERVES 6

1/2 cup fresh lime juice

1/2 cup chopped fresh cilantro

1/2 cup olive oil

1/3 cup soy sauce

1/4 cup tequila

8 garlic cloves, crushed

2 teaspoons grated lime zest

2 teaspoons ground cumin

2 teaspoons dried oregano

1 teaspoon freshly
ground black pepper

Two 1 1/2-pound
beef loin tri-tip roasts

1. Whisk the lime juice, cilantro, oil, soy sauce, tequila, garlic, lime zest, cumin, oregano, and pepper in a medium bowl. Using a small sharp knife, pierce the meat all over. Place the meat in a large self-sealing plastic bag, and add the marinade. Seal the bag. Refrigerate for at least 2 hours or overnight, turning plastic bag occasionally.

2. Preheat a grill to high heat. Remove the meat from the marinade and grill over direct heat to desired doneness, 10 to 15 minutes per side for medium-rare. Transfer to a cutting board; let rest for 10 minutes. Cut diagonally across the grain.

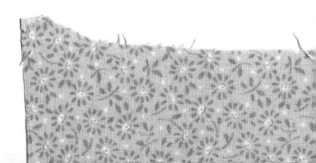

Three-Way Filet

Whether you prefer the rich flavors and textures of Gorgonzola Sauce (facing page), Béarnaise Sauce (page 54), or Basil Compound Butter (page 55), when slathered over a tenderloin steak, these sauces create sumptuous pairings not to be missed. Gemma prepared all three sauces once, and we savored each one. The Meat Club recommends using filet mignon steaks for a truly decadent experience, but other tenderloin steaks and sirloin steaks such as New York strip, T-bone, and porterhouse are also delicious.

SERVES 4

Four 6-ounce beef filets

2 tablespoons unsalted butter, softened

Salt

Freshly ground black pepper

1. Preheat the oven to 500°F.

2. Cover the meat on both sides with the butter and sprinkle evenly with salt and pepper. Place on baking sheet and roast for 10 to 12 minutes for rare and 15 to 18 minutes for medium-rare.

3. Remove the beef from the oven, cover with foil, and allow to rest at room temperature for at least 5 minutes before serving with any or all of the sauces.

Gorgonzola Sauce

This lovely sauce takes a little patience (45 minutes of patience) but it is well worth it. Keep this in mind when timing your steaks. If you finish the cream first, it can sit on low heat until steaks are ready. The more you simmer it, the richer it will be!

MAKES 1 CUP

2 cups heavy cream

1/2 cup (4 ounces) crumbled Gorgonzola cheese

2 tablespoons chopped fresh parsley

3 tablespoons grated Parmesan cheese

1/2 teaspoon salt

1/2 teaspoon freshly ground black pepper

1. In a saucepan over medium-high heat, bring the cream to a boil. Reduce the heat to low and simmer for 40 minutes, until creamy.

2. Remove the cream from the heat and add the Gorgonzola, parsley, Parmesan, salt, and pepper.

3. Whisk the sauce rapidly until smooth and set on low heat until ready to serve.

Béarnaise Sauce

Made with butter and eggs with a hint of fresh tarragon, this velvety sauce is typically served over steak in France. We added the Tabasco sauce to ours for a little extra American kick.

MAKES 2¹/₂ CUPS

1 cup white wine

2 shallots, chopped

Leaves from 6 sprigs fresh tarragon or 1 tablespoon dried tarragon

1 tablespoon tarragon vinegar (optional)

4 egg yolks

1 tablespoon warm water

2 cups (4 sticks) butter, melted

3 teaspoons green Tabasco sauce

Salt

Freshly ground black pepper

1. In a saucepan, combine the wine, shallots, tarragon, and vinegar (if using).

2. Bring to a simmer over medium heat and reduce by three-quarters, 10 to 15 minutes. Remove from the heat and let cool.

3. In a blender, mix the egg yolks and water.

4. Add the reduced wine mixture to the eggs while the blender is running.

5. With the blender on lowest speed, slowly add the melted butter until blended.

6. Pour the sauce into a medium bowl, stir in the Tabasco, and add salt and pepper to taste.

Juicy Tidbit: This sauce will keep well for up to 3 days in the refrigerator. Spread leftovers on bread or crackers for a truly decadent experience!

Basil Compound Butter

The ancient Romans thought that the smell of basil inspired love. A woman seeking love needed only to give the object of her affection a sprig of basil and he was hers forever. Wouldn't that be nice? A taste of this basil butter might actually make your object of affection swoon. The butter will keep, wrapped and stored in the refrigerator, for up to five days.

The easiest and most efficient way to cut basil is to stack the leaves on top of one another and roll into a tight cylinder. Slice the leaves cross-wise into thin strips. You'll notice that you have perfectly cut pieces of basil ready to use. This is called *chiffonade.*

MAKES ½ CUP

8 tablespoons (1 stick) unsalted butter, softened

1 bunch chiffonaded fresh basil

1 tablespoon minced garlic

Salt

Freshly ground black pepper

1. Cut the butter into small pieces.

2. In a small bowl, mix the butter with the basil and garlic.

3. Add salt and pepper to taste.

4. Slather over cooked steaks.

Paris-in-Love Steak au Poivre

One of our Meat Club girlfriends, Leslie, first had this steak when she lived in Paris as a child. This recipe was adapted from a recipe in a French cookbook by Raymond Olivier that Leslie's mother brought back from France. Most recipes for Steak au Poivre call for black peppercorns, but this recipe calls for the more succulent brined green variety. Leslie's mother makes this dish using very tender filet mignon, but a nice flavorful New York steak is a good alternative. This recipe calls for a fancy flambé (which is simply lighting a flame to the pan), so make this dish for friends who like food with flare.

SERVES 4

Four 6-ounce steaks, preferably filet mignon or other tender loin or sirloin steaks

Salt

1 tablespoon butter

1/2 tablespoon olive oil

1/2 cup cognac or brandy

1 cup crème fraîche or heavy whipping cream

1/4 cup brined green peppercorns, drained

1. Pat the steaks dry with a paper towel and season generously with salt.

2. In a large skillet or sauté pan, heat the butter and oil over medium-high heat.

3. Add the steaks to the skillet and cook 5 minutes per side for rare or to your taste. Remove the steaks to a platter and set aside.

4. Pour off grease from the pan and return to the stove top. Pour in the cognac and heat for 1 minute.

5. Remove the pan from the heat and very carefully light the cognac with a match to flambé it (burn off the alcohol).

6. Return to the heat and stir in the crème fraîche. Cook over low heat until thickened, about 5 minutes. Add in the peppercorns, any meat juices from the platter, and salt to taste.

7. Plate the steaks and sauce them generously.

Steak Pizzaiola

Gemma's mother was known as "the converted Italian." She is Irish born but when she married Gemma's Italian father, he taught her how to cook like a true Italian. Steak Pizzaiola (which means "baked with tomato sauce") was one of the meals she mastered. We think that she makes it better than he does now! We recommend using the less expensive but flavorful chuck steaks, as the meat will be tenderized from braising in the sauce, but you can also use a rib-eye or sirloin. Serve with a simple butter lettuce salad with fresh lemon juice and olive oil drizzled on top and a piece of warm Italian bread.

SERVES 4

4 tablespoons olive oil

1 onion, minced

2 tablespoons crushed garlic

One 28-ounce can crushed tomatoes

1/4 cup red wine

1 teaspoon salt

1 teaspoon pepper

1 tablespoon minced fresh parsley

Two 2-pound chuck steaks

1. Preheat the oven to 350°F.

2. In an ovenproof sauté pan or skillet, heat 2 tablespoons of the oil over medium heat.

3. Add the onion and garlic and sauté until soft, about 5 minutes.

4. Add the tomatoes, red wine, salt, pepper, and parsley and let simmer and reduce for 20 minutes over low heat.

5. Transfer the tomato mixture into a bowl.

6. In the same pan over medium heat, add the remaining 2 tablespoons oil. When the oil is heated, add the steaks and cook for 3 to 4 minutes on each side. The steaks should be brown on each side but not cooked through the center.

7. Pour the tomato mixture over the steaks and place in the oven.

8. Braise for 30 minutes, or until the sauce is baked nicely on the steaks. Halve each steak and serve it with some of the sauce.

Sassy Beef Satay with Peanut Sauce

Every summer, Kristina attends a family picnic thrown by her in-laws. It is a huge gathering with up to ten barbecues going at once. One of her favorite dishes is this beef satay, made by her mother-in-law, Vicky. All the cousins, aunts, uncles, and other far-flung relatives, young and old, come running when Vicky offers up these sassy satays. Flank steak is ideal for this recipe because it is extremely tasty and threads easily on skewers. The Meat Club adapted this recipe for the broiler, but feel free to throw the skewers on a hot grill. Serve with the refreshing Pickled Cucumber Salad.

SERVES 4 TO 6

1½ pounds flank steak

Marinade

2 scallions, chopped

¼ cup teriyaki sauce

¼ cup sesame oil

2 tablespoons chopped peeled fresh ginger

1 large garlic clove, crushed

½ teaspoon kosher salt

½ teaspoon freshly ground black pepper

1. Cut the steak across the grain into ¼-inch-thick slices

2. To make the marinade: Add all of the ingredients to a large self-sealing plastic bag. Add the meat, seal the bag, and marinate at room temperature for 30 minutes or refrigerate for up to 1 hour.

3. To make the Cucumber Salad: Peel the cucumbers, slice into ¼-inch rounds, and place in a medium bowl. Combine with the vinegar, basil, and salt and pepper to taste. Toss lightly. Refrigerate for 1 hour before serving.

4. To make the Peanut Sauce: Heat the peanut butter over low heat in a small saucepan.

5. Slowly drizzle in the oil while stirring. Once combined, add the honey, curry paste, and soy sauce.

Pickled Cucumber Salad

4 lemon cucumbers
or 2 waxy cucumbers

³/₄ cup rice wine vinegar

6 large leaves fresh basil,
cut into chiffonade (see page 55)

Salt

Freshly ground black pepper

Peanut Sauce

³/₄ cup smooth peanut butter

¹/₄ cup canola oil or vegetable oil

3 tablespoons honey

2 tablespoons
Thai yellow curry paste

1 tablespoon soy sauce

Fifteen 8-inch wood skewers

6. Place the Peanut Sauce in a bowl and set aside.

7. Preheat the broiler. Thread the strips of meat onto the skewers and place on a broiling pan.

8. Place the skewers under the heat, turning once, until sizzling, cooked through, and browned all over, 6 to 7 minutes. Transfer the skewers to a large platter and serve hot with the Peanut Sauce and Cucumber Salad.

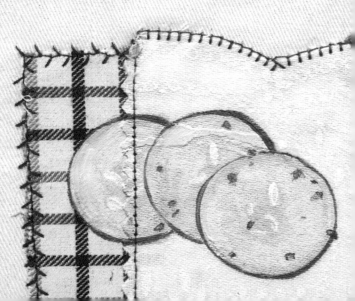

Drunken Beef

This recipe was given to the Meat Club by our dear girlfriend France, who incidentally comes from France. We made this beef bourguignonne stew with France's mother, who has been making this traditional French stew for over thirty years. Though France's mom didn't speak a word of English, Vanessa's high school French and a bottle of wine provided enough common language to collaborate on a great stew.

This cold-weather meal gets better the longer it sits. In this recipe we have incorporated two types of stewing meat for richer flavor—the classic stewing beef from the chuck and the famously tender top sirloin. Let your butcher know and he can cube your pieces in advance.

SERVES 8

3 tablespoons unsalted butter

8 ounces bacon

2½ pounds top sirloin, cut into 1-inch cubes

2½ pounds chuck, cut into 1-inch pieces

1 tablespoon flour

One 750-milliliter bottle Pinot Noir or Burgundy wine

1. Melt the butter in a large cast-iron casserole over medium heat. Add the bacon and brown for approximately 5 minutes until softened, but not crispy. Remove the bacon and save for another use (see Juicy Tidbit).

2. In the same pan, cook the meat in batches until browned evenly, 4 to 5 minutes per side. Once browned, return all the meat to the pan and sprinkle the flour over it. Mix well.

3. Add the wine to cover the meat.

4. Add the carrots, onions, garlic, thyme, and bay leaves. Stir.

10 carrots, peeled and chopped into 1 1/2-inch pieces

12 pearl onions

1 garlic clove, minced

1 1/2 teaspoons dried thyme

2 bay leaves

Salt

Freshly ground black pepper

5. Cover and cook over low to medium heat for 2 hours. The meat should be tender enough to cut with a fork. Add salt and pepper to taste.

Juicy Tidbit: Meat Girls wouldn't be caught dead throwing away bacon! Make a tasty Bacon, Basil, and Apple sandwich (see page 104).

Beef 'n' Beer Stew

The recipe, inspired by Vanessa's years in Manchester, England, is a sophisticated version of a pub favorite. The prunes and spices add a contemporary twist to a classic stew. A great-quality stout beer is a must for this recipe. We gals recommend using our favorite, Guinness. Any cut of stew meat works well for this recipe but if possible, ask your butcher to cut up a chunk of boneless meat from the chuck, such as a blade pot roast, for a truly saucy stew.

SERVES 6

2 pounds lean stewing beef, cut into 1-inch cubes

2 tablespoons flour

Salt

Freshly ground black pepper

2 tablespoons olive oil

1 pound carrots, peeled and sliced into large chunks

3 onions, sliced

2 garlic cloves, crushed

1 1/2 cups beef broth

1 cup stout beer (preferably Guinness)

1 teaspoon allspice berries

1 teaspoon juniper berries

6 cloves

4 ounces (1/2 cup) pitted prunes

Chopped fresh parsley for garnish

1. Preheat the oven to 300°F.

2. In a large bowl, toss the meat with the flour, 1/4 teaspoon salt, and 1/4 teaspoon pepper until evenly coated.

3. In a large sauté pan or skillet, heat the oil over medium heat and add the meat in batches, cooking until browned on all sides. Transfer the meat to a large casserole dish and set aside.

4. To the pan add the carrots, onions, and garlic and cook until brown. Stir in any remaining flour from the meat bowl. Add the broth, then remove the pan from the heat and add the beer off heat to prevent foaming.

5. Return the pan to the heat and, stirring constantly, bring the sauce to a boil.

6. Using a mortar and pestle or spice grinder, roughly crush the allspice berries, juniper berries, and cloves and add to the mixture. Add salt and pepper to taste. Stir in the prunes and pour the mixture into the casserole dish. Cover and bake for 2 to 2 1/2 hours, or until the meat is tender. Garnish with fresh parsley.

Garlic-Infused Rib-Eye Roast

Garlic lovers rejoice! Before our Meat Club days, pleasing finicky eaters at our dinner party meant avoiding not only meat, but also pungent flavors. This rich, robust recipe is an act of celebratory rebellion on our part where we indulge—pairing a tender rib-eye roast with one of our favorite flavors: GARLIC!!!

One of the most flavorful and popular boneless roasts, the rib-eye makes an excellent dish with very little waste. The roast is best when marinated for at least two hours.

SERVES 6

7 garlic cloves,
2 minced and 5 thinly sliced

2 tablespoons olive oil

2 tablespoons soy sauce

2 tablespoons
crushed black peppercorns

1½ tablespoons salt

1 tablespoon finely
chopped fresh rosemary

One 3-pound boneless
rib-eye beef roast

1. In a food processor, combine the minced garlic with the oil, soy sauce, peppercorns, salt, and rosemary and process to a paste. Set aside.

2. Using the tip of a sharp knife, make fifteen 1-inch-deep cuts in the top and bottom of the roast. Insert a thin slice of garlic in each cut. Set the roast on a rack in a roasting pan and rub it all over with the paste. Let stand at room temperature for 2 hours.

3. Preheat the oven to 500°F. Roast the meat for about 10 minutes, or until the crust begins to brown. Reduce the temperature to 350°F and cook for about 1¼ hours longer, or until an instant-read thermometer inserted in the thickest part of the meat registers 125°F for medium-rare.

4. Transfer the roast to a carving board and let rest, uncovered, for 10 minutes. Carve the roast into ½-inch-thick slices.

Hankee Pankee Yankee Pot Roast

We all grew up on the East Coast, where this classic, rich meal satisfied our souls during the cold winter months. The Meat Club updated this dish by adding red wine, garlic, and our secret ingredient, Chinese chili sauce. We use Heavenly Chef's Hunan Red Chili Sauce, but any good chili sauce will do. Though this dish takes two and a half hours to cook, the actual preparation time takes only twenty to thirty minutes, leaving plenty of time for hankee pankee!

All cuts from the chuck make great pot roasts. Be sure to use firm waxy potatoes such as fingerlings or Yukon golds that will stand up to the high oven temperature. The Basil Parsley Pesto (recipe follows) makes a vibrant flavorful accompaniment.

SERVES 6

1/4 cup olive oil

One 3 1/2-pound boneless chuck roast, such as the chuck-eye roast or blade pot roast

Salt

Freshly ground black pepper

6 tablespoons (3/4 stick) unsalted butter

3 medium onions, coarsely chopped

6 large carrots, peeled and thickly sliced

3 medium celery ribs, thickly sliced

1: Preheat the oven to 350°F.

2. Heat the oil over medium heat in a large enameled cast-iron casserole.

3. Season the roast generously with salt and pepper and add it to the casserole.

4. Brown the meat all over, 10 to 12 minutes. Transfer the roast to a platter and set aside.

5. Melt the butter in the casserole. Add the onions, carrots, and celery and sauté over medium heat, stirring until softened, about 5 minutes. Add the garlic and sauté until fragrant, about 2 minutes. Sprinkle in the flour and cook, stirring until incorporated, about 1 minute. Gradually stir in the broth, wine, and water. Add the tomatoes and juice, chili sauce, and sugar and bring to a simmer.

3 large garlic cloves, crushed

¹/₄ cup all-purpose flour

2 cups canned beef broth

2 cups red wine

1 cup water

One 8-ounce can diced Italian plum tomatoes, with their juices

1 tablespoon Chinese hot chili sauce

Pinch of sugar

1 pound firm waxy potatoes, such as Yukon golds, quartered

6. Return the roast to the casserole. Cover and bake for 2 hours, turning it halfway through. Add the potatoes, cover, and cook for an additional 30 minutes, or until the meat and potatoes are fork-tender but not falling apart.

7. Transfer the roast to a cutting board and cover loosely with foil. Using a slotted spoon, transfer the vegetables to a large deep platter, reserving the sauce in the casserole. Cut the meat across the grain into thick slices and arrange on a platter with the vegetables. Season the sauce with salt and pepper and pour over the meat and vegetables before serving. Dollop with the Basil Parsley Pesto, if desired.

MAKES 1 CUP

1 cup shredded fresh basil

1 cup chopped fresh parsley

¹/₂ cup olive oil

3 tablespoons pine nuts

1 garlic clove, minced

Salt

Freshly ground black pepper

Basil Parsley Pesto

Place all the ingredients in a food processor and process until well blended.

Slow-Lovin' Beef Brisket

This recipe was given to us by Erica Holland-Toll, a former chef at the Acme Chop House in San Francisco. The Meat Club loves a traditional chophouse that uses naturally raised meats and sustainably grown produce. We also love a good brisket cooked for endless hours. This recipe takes up to six hours, but if we're too lazy to cook we'll treat ourselves to a night out at Acme. This brisket recipe is easy to carve and goes well with buttered egg noodles and sautéed spinach.

SERVES 4 TO 6

Kosher salt

Freshly ground black pepper

One 6- to 8-pound beef brisket, trimmed of external fat

4 yellow onions, chopped

6 Roma tomatoes, quartered

4 carrots, peeled and chopped into 1-inch pieces

10 garlic cloves

1 bunch fresh thyme, leaves removed

4 bay leaves

1/4 cup olive oil

3 cups red wine

1. Preheat the oven to 500°F.

2. Liberally salt and pepper the brisket.

3. In a large bowl, toss the onions, tomatoes, carrots, garlic, thyme, and bay leaves with the oil, 1 tablespoon salt, and 2 teaspoons pepper. Spread the mixture in a large roasting pan. Place the seasoned brisket on top of the vegetables. (There should be enough room for everything, but the veggies should peek out only an inch or so around the brisket; if they are too spread out they will burn.)

4. Roast for 10 to 20 minutes, until the meat is golden brown all over. Reduce the heat to 275°F and add the wine to the pan. Cook for 8 more minutes and then cover the roasting pan with a tight-fitting lid or aluminum foil.

5. After 3 hours, check the brisket by inserting a knife into the thickest part of the meat. While the brisket should not fall apart, the knife should meet little or no resistance. If it is not yet tender, continue cooking, checking every 20 minutes until done.

6. Carefully remove the meat from the pan, place on a deep platter, and let rest for 10 minutes. With a large spoon, transfer the vegetables and wine to a blender and add any accumulated juices from the resting brisket. Blend until smooth, taste, and adjust for salt and pepper (if it is too thick, add water or chicken stock until desired consistency is found).

7. Slice the brisket against the grain, arrange on a shallow platter, and pour the sauce over. The brisket can be cooled at this point and reheated in the oven later as needed.

Not-So-Classic Osso Bucco

This dish from the Piedmont region in Italy typically uses veal shank, but we use beef shanks in our version. Beef shanks are often overlooked but quite tasty when slow cooked. Braised in a fragrant mix of tomatoes, garlic, and orange zest, the meat is tender enough to cut with a fork. Like most stews, osso bucco gets better with time. You'll want to make an extra batch for yourself and the girls to enjoy eating all week long. *Gremolata* is a garnish traditionally made with fresh parsley, garlic, and lemon peel. It is sprinkled over Osso Bucco and rubbed on meats for a fresh, sprightly flavor.

SERVES 6

¼ cup flour

Salt

Freshly ground black pepper

6 pounds beef shanks, cut in 1½-inch slices

2 tablespoons olive oil

2 tablespoons butter

2 onions, chopped

3 carrots, peeled and chopped

½ bottle (about 1½ cups) dry white wine

Two 14-ounce cans plum tomatoes, chopped

1. Preheat the oven to 350°F. Put the flour on a plate, add generous amounts of salt and pepper, and coat the shanks with flour. Heat the oil and butter in a large (at least 6-quart) ovenproof casserole over medium heat. Add half the shanks and brown them, 2 to 3 minutes. Turn them, browning all sides, and remove them to a plate. Repeat with the remaining shanks.

2. Lower the heat to medium, add the onions and carrots, and sauté until golden, 5 to 7 minutes. Pour in the wine and boil until reduced by half, stirring to dissolve the pan juices. Stir in the tomatoes, 1 cup stock, garlic, orange and lemon zests, and salt and pepper to taste. Immerse the shanks in the sauce; the liquid should come at least halfway up the sides. Cover the pan and bring to a boil.

3. Braise the shanks in the oven until the meat is very tender and falling from the bone, 1½ to 2 hours. Stir from time to time,

1 cup veal, beef,
or chicken stock,
plus more if needed

3 garlic cloves, chopped

Grated zest of 2 oranges

Grated zest of 1 lemon

Gremolata

½ bunch fresh
flat-leaf parsley

½ bunch fresh basil

3 or 4 garlic cloves,
chopped

Grated zest of 1 orange

Grated zest of 1 lemon

gently turning the shanks, and if the pan seems dry, add more stock. At the end of cooking, taste and adjust the seasoning of the sauce.

4. Meanwhile, make the *Gremolata:* Pull the parsley and basil leaves from the stems and chop the leaves with the garlic. Stir in the grated zests and pile the *Gremolata* on top of the hot Osso Bucco once served.

Blazin' Asian Short Ribs

Vanessa's Korean aunt, Janette, is the inspiration for this dish. Short ribs
are Korea's national meat—they are great for stewing, grilling, and simmering. Beef ribs are cut in two different styles: English style and Flanken
style. English-style ribs are rectangular in appearance and include a bit of
the rib or are boneless. Flanken-style ribs are cut parallel to the bone. We
prefer the English style for this recipe because they are slightly meatier.
Marinating the meat for two hours or even overnight makes this recipe
rich with flavor. The Asian pears and chili sauce give these saucy ribs a
sweet spicy kick. If you don't have Asian pears, you can substitute a ripe,
firm variety of pear such as Bosc.

SERVES 6

4 pounds meaty beef short ribs,
preferably English style

3 scallions, thinly sliced

1/4 cup sugar

1/4 cup Korean rice wine vinegar

3 tablespoons Asian sesame oil

2 tablespoons minced garlic

2 tablespoons sesame salt
(see Juicy Tidbit)

1 tablespoon vegetable oil

1. Using a sharp knife, score the ribs on both
sides. In a large bowl, mix the scallions with
the sugar, vinegar, sesame oil, garlic, and
sesame salt. Add the short ribs and toss to
coat evenly. Cover and refrigerate for at least
2 hours or overnight.

2. Scrape the marinade off the meat and
reserve. Heat the vegetable oil over medium
heat in a large enameled cast-iron casserole.
Add half of the short ribs, brown about 5 minutes per side, and transfer the browned ribs
to a plate. Repeat with the remaining ribs,
adjusting the heat as necessary if the juices
on the bottom of the casserole get too dark.

3. Add the carrots and pears to the casserole
and cook for 3 minutes, stirring frequently.
Return the ribs to the casserole. Add the
water, soy sauce, chili sauce, and reserved
marinade and bring to a boil, skimming fat as
necessary. Cover the casserole and simmer
over low heat until the ribs are tender, about
1 1/2 hours.

4 medium carrots,
peeled and cut
into 1-inch pieces

2 large Asian pears,
halved, cored, and cut
into 1½-inch chunks

4 cups water

½ cup soy sauce

1 tablespoon Chinese
hot chili sauce

Toasted sesame
seeds for garnish

4. Using a slotted spoon, transfer the ribs, vegetables, and pears to a bowl and cover to keep warm. Simmer the sauce in the casserole over medium heat until thickened and richly flavored, about 20 minutes. Return the ribs, carrots, and pears to the sauce and simmer until warmed through. Serve the ribs in large shallow bowls and garnish with the sesame seeds.

Juicy Tidbit: Sesame salt, or *gomasio,* has excellent flavor and can be found at most supermarkets. It adds a unique taste and is a great substitute for plain salt.

Momma's Liver Roll-Ups

O.K., liver roll-ups—I know what you're thinking . . . yuck! But this isn't like the liver your mom used to serve you as a child. It's sweet and savory and surprisingly delicious, and best served as an appetizer. Vanessa's mother made these tasty little treats at every family get-together and they would go like hot cakes! Vanessa's mom prefers to use the George Foreman Grill, but they work just as well in the oven on a baking sheet.

SERVES 10 TO 12

2 pounds beef livers, cut into 1-inch pieces

One 32-ounce can pineapple chunks, drained

1 pound bacon strips, halved

1. Preheat the oven to 425°F.

2. Take 1 piece of liver and place it next to a chunk of pineapple on the end of a strip of bacon. Roll up and place on a non-stick baking sheet. Repeat with the remaining liver, pineapple, and bacon, placing the roll-ups on the baking sheet at least 1 inch apart.

3. Bake for 20 minutes, or until the bacon is cooked and slightly crispy. Place a toothpick in the center of each one and serve.

Chapter Three
Pretty in Pork

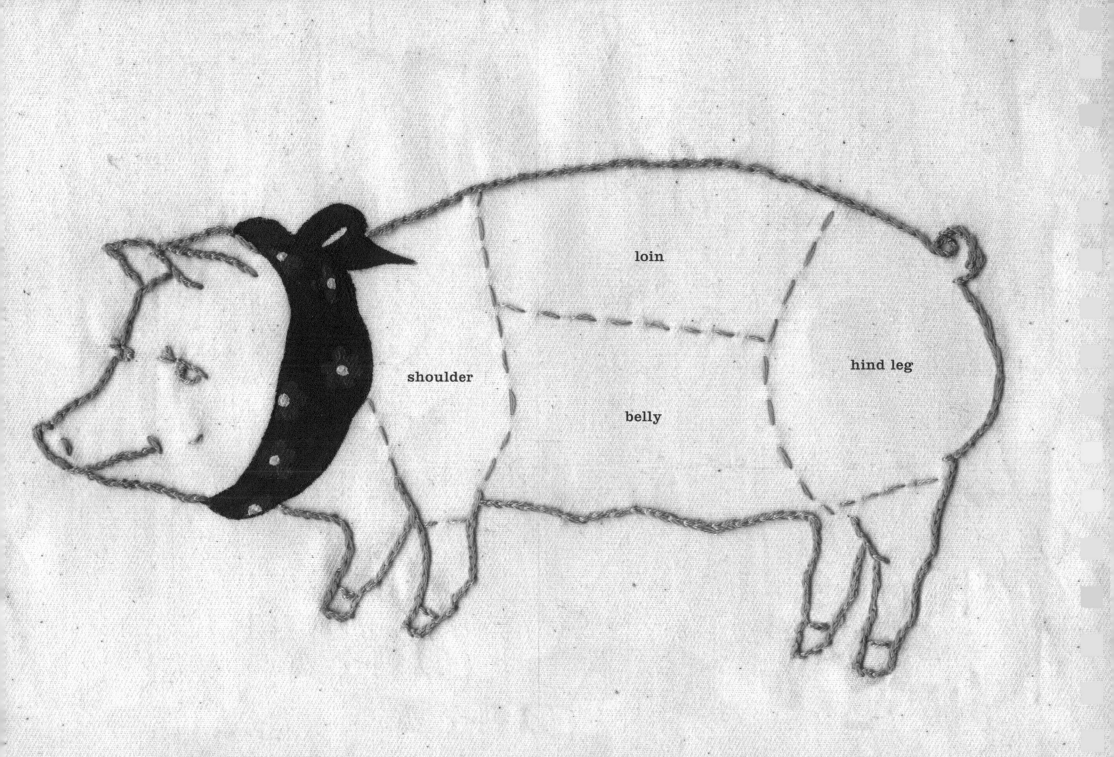

We love pork. It's cute (or at least the pig is), cheap, and pink! In fact, on our very first Meat Club night, we ate pork tenderloin with orange sauce. Since that time, we've fallen in love with all the possibilities the pig has to offer: pan-roasted double-cut pork chops, quick-cooked thin pork cutlets, festive baked hams, slow-cooked spareribs—the list goes on. And, of course, everything tastes better with bacon.

As you can see, pork is versatile. The pig is also relatively easy to raise—relative to the cow, that is—which means that pigs are nearly everywhere. That translates into pork recipes in kitchens around the globe. Pork's mild flavor, another plus, guarantees that it pairs easily with flavors great and small: spices, herbs, vegetables, and especially fruits.

Pork is also excellent combined with salt and smoke. When cured to create ham or bacon, pork takes on a sublime flavor that has caused the downfall of a number of vegetarians we know. We can easily conceive of eating a whole side of bacon any time, any day. Prosciutto, pancetta, salt pork, salami, bacon, and country ham—they are all fabulous and we use them early and often to add salt, smoke, and flavor to stews, pastas, soups, and sandwiches.

The secret to great pork is to cook it quickly and halt cooking when the meat is still nice and pink. In the past, people thought they needed to cook pork until it was well done (160°F), because of the fear of trichinosis. But now eating pork cooked medium (145°F) is widely considered safe, since those nasty little microscopic parasites are sent to their final resting place at 137°F. Of course, the fattier cuts, such as shoulder and ham, will stay moist and develop flavor when cooked for longer.

As with talk, pork is cheap. Indeed, next to poultry, it's the bargain of the butcher counter. This is especially handy if you have a big bunch of girls to feed and you don't want to break the piggy bank. You can grill up a rib feast or bake a ham for twelve and still have some cash for that pair of shoes you've been eyeing at the local Prada outlet. So bring on the bacon, bring on the baby backs, and bring on the power of pork!

The Meaty Basics: Pork

Making the Grade
Unlike beef and lamb, pork has a grading system that's easy to remember. It's based on numbers, with Grade 1 being the best quality and Grade 4 the poorest. However, you'd never know that pork had multiple grades because most stores carry only Grade 1 pork. Count yourself lucky that even though you have no choice, you do have the best.

You've Got the Look
Reach for pretty reddish pink meat that is firm, slightly moist, and has a fine grain. The cut should include a moderate amount of creamy white, firm, smooth fat. Avoid meat that is pale, looks watery, or promises to make your cholesterol spike.

Favorite Flavorings
Dunking your pork into a salt brine is a good way to keep it nice and juicy. We also love to slather our pork with dry rubs and to marinate and sauce pork with such sweet and savory ingredients as honey, wine, brandy, citrus, fresh herbs, mustard, garlic, and dried and fresh fruits such as apricots, prunes, and raisins.

Cook It Right
We love all things pink, especially our pork. An instant-read thermometer and your eyes are the key to checking pork doneness. Perfectly done pork should have a pale pink center. For chops and cutlets, you can check pinkness by simply cutting into the center. When using an instant-read thermometer for roasts and thicker cuts, keep in mind that the temperature can rise between 5 and 10 degrees during resting, so remove it from the heat slightly before it reaches the right temperature.

Most chops, steaks, tenderloins, and ribs are delicious sautéed, grilled, broiled, or pan roasted. Be sure to cook chops, steaks, and other thin flat cuts quickly over high heat. Cooked too long on too low a heat, the juices will exude and leave you with dry meat. Center-cut loins are tasty roasted in the oven, while fattier cuts such as the Boston butt (shoulder) and the blade end of the loin should be stewed or braised. Remember that long-cooked pork is never as tender as its beef or lamb counterparts.

Storing Pork

Store fresh pork for no more than four days; pork sausage for no more than five days; and bacon and ham for no more than seven days. Freeze pork for no more than six months.

The Mystique of the Pig Physique

The pig is divided into four primal cuts (see figure on fold-out): the shoulder, loin, belly, and hind leg, each with its own attributes.

SHOULDER: When we need a shoulder to cry on, we look to pork shoulder for support. The shoulder contains some of the best meat to stew, roast, or braise, including the Boston butt (in Boston they must not know which end is up) and the picnic ham, also known as the front leg. Both cuts are big and fatty and are cooked for big groups. The shoulder also sports some steaks and chops, including the pork blade steak and the split blade chop, which can be tough but are great for stews. Those ultra-thin pork cutlets, also known as scallops or scaloppine, great breaded for a quick sauté, are cut from the sirloin end of the leg.

LOIN: Just like with beef and lamb, we love the loin! The pork loin contains some of the most valuable and tender roasting meat on the pig as well as the best ribs and chops.

For roasts, the loin contains our all-time favorite, the tenderloin. With a weight that ranges from three-fourths to one and a half pounds, it is ideal for a dinner for one with leftovers if you grab a small one, or for a small party of three or four if you grab a hefty one. It's quite lean, so you must be careful not to overcook it. (You can also cut the tenderloin into medallions and sauté them.) There are also loin roasts, both bone in and boneless, variously labeled the rib end (from the shoulder end), the rump end (from the rear end), and the center loin, center-cut loin, or center-cut rib. All these roasts may also be cut into chops. Boneless center-cut loin is smoked to make Canadian bacon.

Baby back ribs and country-style ribs are also from the loin (though neither are really ribs at all but are cut into ribs). Small and meaty, baby backs are great barbecued or broiled. Country-style ribs are inexpensive and more fatty and do nicely when slow grilled or braised.

Our favorite chops also come from the loin. We like center-cut loin chops that have an "eye" of meat at least an inch thick. We also like rib chops (cut from the loin), loin chops, and sirloin chops, all of which have great flavor and tenderness.

BELLY: Salted belly is salt pork; smoked belly is bacon. And you know how we feel about bacon. Need we say more? The belly also includes the spareribs, which, as far as we're concerned, are the best ribs of all. Spareribs are best cooked slowly, to render their fat and make them tender. It's a good idea to put them on a grill over indirect heat until the meat is so tender it's nearly ready to fall off the bone.

HIND LEG: When we want to ham it up, we reach for the hind leg. Hams are sold fresh, cured, and smoked. (The term *ham* refers to the back leg of the pig, whether it is cured or fresh.) Although we rarely, if ever, cook them, ham steaks include the pork scallop and the fresh ham steak. Some butchers round off pieces of fresh ham to create fresh ham steaks that we like to cook just like beef steaks.

So, whether you light up the grill and dress your spareribs with our secret sauce (page 100) or turn on the oven for our famous Asian-inspired Sweet Honey Pork Roast (page 86), you are sure to become a champion of all things pork.

Easy-Bake Spareribs

Remember your Easy-Bake Oven as a little girl? Well, this recipe is just as simple as that and just as good as ribs on the grill. Baby back ribs aren't really ribs (they are taken from the upper section of the loin), but they are smaller and take less time to cook than other rib cuts. While maybe we shy away from licking our fingers and gnawing on the bone in mixed crowds, these ribs are perfect for the Meat Club!

SERVES 4 TO 6

¾ cup sugar

½ cup soy sauce

½ cup ketchup

¼ cup medium-dry sherry

1 teaspoon salt

1 garlic clove, smashed

One 1-inch cube peeled fresh ginger, crushed

3 pounds baby back pork ribs (3 racks; do not cut apart)

1. Stir together the sugar, soy sauce, ketchup, sherry, and salt in a medium bowl until the sugar is dissolved. Pour the marinade into a roasting pan; add the garlic, ginger, and ribs, turning ribs to coat them with marinade.

2. Marinate, covered and refrigerated, turning occasionally, at least 3 hours.

3. Preheat the oven to 325°F.

4. Line the bottom of a broiler pan with foil and arrange the ribs rounded sides up on the broiler rack, reserving the marinade for basting. Bake in the middle of the oven, basting with the marinade every 20 minutes (do not baste during last 10 minutes of cooking), until the ribs are tender and the glaze is well browned, about 1¾ hours. Discard any unused marinade.

5. Let the racks stand 5 minutes, then cut into individual ribs and serve immediately.

Love Me Tender Pork Tenderloin

This is one of the very first dishes served at the Meat Club, and it remains one of our favorites. We serve the pork sliced over a bed of pistachio couscous and topped with sautéed fennel and roasted corn. Center-cut pork tenderloin can be pan roasted or sautéed first, then finished off in the oven. We finish ours in the oven to make use of our tasty marinade by adding it to the pan juices for a delightful sauce.

SERVES 4

2 pounds pork tenderloin

1 cup red wine, preferably Merlot or Cabernet

1 cup fresh orange juice

5 fresh basil leaves, torn into small pieces (optional)

1 tablespoon orange zest

1 tablespoon freshly ground black pepper

1 teaspoon garlic powder or 1 garlic clove, crushed

2 tablespoons olive oil

Salt

Freshly ground black pepper

1. Place the pork, wine, orange juice, basil (if using), orange zest, pepper, and garlic in a large, heavy-duty self-sealing plastic bag and marinate in the refrigerator for at least 4 hours.

2. Preheat the oven to 350°F.

3. Remove the pork from the bag and reserve the marinade.

4. Heat the oil in a large sauté pan or skillet over medium heat and add the pork. Brown evenly on all sides, about 5 minutes for each side.

5. Transfer the meat to a roasting pan and bake for about 20 minutes for medium-rare.

6. Meanwhile, in the same pan used for browning the pork, add the reserved marinade and simmer over medium heat until the pork is ready. Season with salt and pepper.

7. Transfer the pork to a cutting board and let rest for at least 5 minutes before slicing. Serve with the marinade reduction.

Fruit of the Loin

Pork and dried fruit, especially prunes, is a classic combination. Cut from the tenderloin, pork medallions are fast and a breeze to cook. This dish makes an ideal weekday meal for friends and family.

SERVES 4

1 tablespoon olive oil, plus more if needed

1 pound pork tenderloin, cut into four 1-inch-thick medallions

Salt

Freshly ground black pepper

1 onion, finely chopped

2 garlic cloves, minced

1/2 cup dry red wine

1/2 cup canned low-sodium chicken broth or homemade stock

1 tablespoon tomato paste

4 tablespoons chopped fresh parsley

12 pitted prunes

1. In a large sauté pan or skillet, heat the 1 tablespoon oil over medium heat. Season the medallions with 1/4 teaspoon each salt and pepper. Place in the pan. Cook, turning once, until browned and done to medium, about 3 minutes per side. Remove and put on a warm plate.

2. If necessary, add oil to the pan to make about 2 tablespoons fat. Add the onion and a generous 1/2 teaspoon salt. Cook, covered, stirring occasionally, until the onion is soft, about 10 minutes. Stir in the garlic, cook for 1 minute longer, and add the wine. Bring the mixture to a boil, scraping the bottom of the pan to dislodge any browned bits. Simmer for 5 to 10 minutes, until the liquid is reduced to approximately 1/4 cup.

3. Stir in the broth, tomato paste, 2 table-spoons of the parsley, and any accumulated juices from the meat. Add the prunes. Bring to a simmer and cook until the sauce thickens and the prunes are soft, about 5 minutes. Add 1 tablespoon of the remaining parsley, 1/8 teaspoon pepper, and the medallions. Cook until just heated through, 1 to 2 minutes. Plate the medallions and spoon the sauce over top, placing 3 prunes on each plate. Finish the dish by sprinkling with the remaining 1 tablespoon parsley and serve immediately.

Peachy Keen Pork Loin with Fresh Peach and Ginger Chutney

We made this dish at the height of summer when the peaches were at their peak and served it up with a sparkling Prosecco and a girly rosé for a lovely light meal. It was so good that we made it again in the winter using frozen peaches. Ask your butcher to butterfly the pork loin for you (slicing it in half lengthwise almost all the way through, leaving a hinge of uncut meat). The spicy Peach and Ginger Chutney adds a little sexy sizzle and will keep refridgerated for up to two weeks.

SERVES 4

Pork Loin

2 pounds boneless pork loin, butterflied

1/2 teaspoon garlic powder

Salt

Freshly ground black pepper

5 thin slices prosciutto

Leaves of 5 sprigs fresh thyme

1 large peach, sliced into 1/4-inch-thick segments, or one 14-ounce bag frozen peaches

3 tablespoons extra-virgin olive oil

1/2 cup chicken stock

1/2 cup dry white wine

1. To make the pork loin, preheat the oven to 400°F. Set the pork loin on a work surface, opening it like a book, with cut sides up. Season the insides generously with the garlic powder and salt and pepper.

2. Cover the pork loin with a single layer of overlapping prosciutto slices; sprinkle the thyme leaves over the slices and arrange the peach slices in a row on top. Roll up the pork loin and tie it with kitchen twine at 1 1/2-inch intervals. Season the outsides of the pork loin generously with salt and pepper.

3. Heat the oil over medium-high heat in a very large ovenproof skillet or sauté pan until shimmering. Add the pork loin and cook, turning as needed, until it is browned all over, about 10 minutes total. Transfer the loin to a large platter.

4. Pour off any fat from the skillet and return it to high heat. Add half of the stock and bring to a boil, scraping up any

Fresh Peach and Ginger Chutney

2 tablespoons olive oil

1 medium red onion, cut into ½-inch dice

2 tablespoons grated peeled fresh ginger

2 peaches (8 ounces), peeled and cut into ½-inch dice

½ cup canned unsweetened pineapple juice

¼ cup cider vinegar

¼ cup packed light brown sugar

½ teaspoon red pepper flakes

Salt

Freshly ground black pepper

browned bits from the bottom of the pan. Return the pork loin to the skillet and roast it in the oven for 40 to 45 minutes, or until an instant-read thermometer inserted in the thickest part of the meat registers 145°F. Transfer the pork loin to a large cutting board, cover loosely with foil, and let stand for 15 minutes.

5. While the pork is roasting, make the chutney: Heat the oil in a large heavy skillet or sauté pan over medium-high heat until hot, then sauté the onion, stirring frequently, until softened. Add the ginger and sauté for 1 minute.

6. Stir in the diced peaches, pineapple juice, vinegar, brown sugar, and red pepper flakes. Simmer, stirring occasionally, until thickened, about 15 minutes. Season to taste with salt and pepper. Remove from the heat and let cool to room temperature. (Makes about 2 cups.)

7. Pour the juices from the pan used to cook the pork into a small saucepan and skim off the fat. Add the remaining stock to the pan and set it over high heat. Add the wine, scrape up any browned bits from the bottom of the pan, and boil until reduced to a few tablespoons. Add the wine mixture to the juices in the saucepan and bring to a boil. Season to taste with salt and pepper.

8. Untie the pork loin and carve the meat into ½-inch-thick slices. Arrange the slices on plates, drizzle with the sauce, and serve with the chutney.

Fennel-Brined Roasted Pork Loin

This is another tasty recipe from Erica Holland-Toll. Brining is an excellent way to keep your pork tender and juicy. This recipe uses a fennel brine. Fennel is a subtle licorice-flavored vegetable that makes for a wonderful complement to the salty pork. You'll need to brine the pork for two days in a container that will fit in your refrigerator, so plan accordingly.

SERVES 6 TO 8

Fennel Brine

1 gallon water

2 yellow onions, sliced

1 cup kosher salt

1 cup sugar

¼ cup freshly ground black pepper

⅓ cup ground fennel seeds

1. To make the Fennel Brine: Combine all the ingredients in a large bowl and mix thoroughly until the salt and sugar are dissolved.

2. Place the pork loin and brine in a two-gallon container or something big enough to submerge the loin completely in brine. Brine, refrigerated, for 2 days.

3. Preheat the oven to 500°F.

4. Place the loin, fat side up, in a roasting pan that is a bit larger than the loin. (If the pan is too large, then juices that accumulate from the roasting process will burn.) Roast for 20 minutes, or until golden brown. Reduce the heat to 400°F and cook for about 40 minutes, or until an instant-read thermometer reads 130°F.

5. Remove the pork loin from the oven and carefully place it on a cutting board. Let rest for 15 minutes.

4 to 6 pounds
boneless pork loin

2 cups white wine

2 cups chicken stock

Salt and freshly
ground black pepper
(optional)

6. When the roasting pan has cooled slightly, remove excess fat and place the pan on the stove top over medium heat. Add the wine and cook until reduced by half, about 15 minutes, scraping off the browned bits from the bottom of the roasting pan until they are incorporated into the wine. Add the stock and reduce by half again, 10 to 15 minutes. Taste and season with salt and pepper, if needed.

7. Slice the loin in ¼-inch medallions, arrange on a serving platter, and spoon the sauce over the top. Serve immediately.

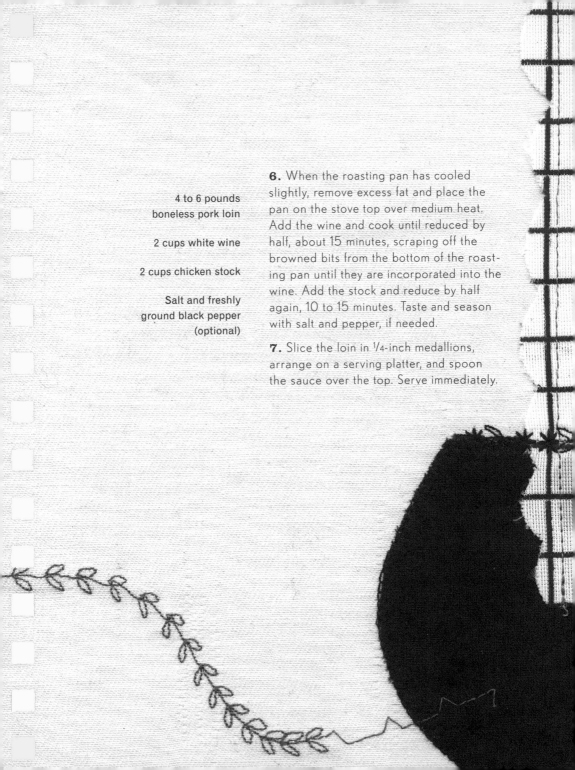

My Sweet Honey Pork Roast with Asian Slaw

When Kristina married into an Asian-Portuguese family, her cooking started to incorporate Asian flavors. Traditional Chinese roast pork is usually made using the pork shoulder, but we prefer the leaner texture and flavor of the boneless sirloin roast or the boneless center-cut pork loin. The sweet and savory flavors will bring your guests to the table like bees to honey. Serve with Asian Slaw.

SERVES 4 TO 6

4 pounds boneless sirloin roast or center-cut pork loin

3/4 cup honey

1/2 cup soy sauce

1/2 cup dry sherry

1/4 cup packed brown sugar

3 garlic cloves, minced

1 teaspoon ground ginger

1. Pierce the meat all over with a fork and place the roast in a large plastic roasting bag. In a medium bowl, combine the honey, soy sauce, sherry, brown sugar, garlic, and ginger. Mix well and pour the mixture into the bag with the pork. Press air out of bag and tie securely. Refrigerate for at least 8 hours or overnight.

2. Meanwhile, make the Asian Slaw: Whisk together the vinegar, brown sugar, and hot sauce in a large bowl and add the cabbage, apple, bell pepper, and cilantro. Mix well to cover the vegetables. Season with salt and pepper. Refrigerate for 4 to 8 hours before serving.

3. Preheat the oven to 325°F.

4. Reserving the marinade, remove the roast and place it in a 9-by-13-inch baking dish. Roast for 50 minutes. Brush with the reserved marinade, cover loosely with foil, and roast for an additional 10 minutes, or until the internal temperature has reached 145°F, brushing several more times with the marinade.

Asian Slaw

½ cup rice wine vinegar

¼ cup packed brown sugar

1 teaspoon hot sauce

½ head green cabbage,
cored and sliced

1 Fuji apple,
cut into 2-inch strips

1 red bell pepper,
cut into 2-inch strips

1 bunch fresh
cilantro, chopped

Salt

Freshly ground black pepper

1 tablespoon cornstarch

1 tablespoon cold water

5. Remove the roast from the oven and let rest for 15 minutes. Combine the pan drippings with the remaining marinade in a saucepan. In a small bowl, combine the cornstarch with the water, mix together, and add the mixture to the marinade. Boil the mixture for 4 to 5 minutes, or until it thickens. Serve with the roast, alongside the Asian Slaw.

Tangy Tarragon Pork Roast

The history of tarragon is linked to dragons because of the way its serpent-shaped stem shoots out roots. In the Middle Ages, there was a widespread belief that tarragon could not only ward off serpents and dragons but also heal snake bites. We love this recipe 'cause it's simple—the way life and dating should be—no matter what dragons or snakes you meet along the way!

This recipes starts on the stove (or grill if you prefer) and finishes in the oven, leaving your stove top free for making savory side dishes. We recommend serving this dish with a crusty French bread and roasted vegetables. The tarragon pesto adds a vibrant splash of green.

SERVES 4 TO 6

3 pounds center-cut pork loin

Salt

Freshly ground black pepper

1 cup olive oil

1. Preheat the oven to 500°F.

2. Season the pork loin with salt and pepper.

3. In a large sauté pan or skillet, heat the olive oil until smoking. Sear the loin for 2 minutes per side, until well browned all over.

4. Remove the loin from the skillet and place on a rack in a roasting pan.

5. Roast for 30 minutes, or until golden brown.

6. Meanwhile, make the Tarrgon Pesto: Blend the tarragon, walnuts, walnut oil, shallot, and garlic together in a food processor until combined. Add salt and pepper to taste.

Tarragon Pesto

1 bunch fresh tarragon

3/4 cup (6 ounces) walnuts

1/4 cup walnut oil

1 shallot, diced

1 garlic clove

Salt

Freshly ground black pepper

1 bunch fresh tarragon, minced

1 cup whole-grain mustard

7. Remove the roast from the oven and reduce the heat to 350°F.

8. Mix together the minced tarragon and mustard and slather it evenly over the roast.

9. Return the roast to the oven and bake for an additional 40 minutes, or until an instant-read thermometer reads 145°F. Remove from the oven and let rest for 10 minutes. Serve with the Pesto.

Pull Out the Stops Pork

Vanessa's first encounter with pulled pork was at Borough Market in London. There was an entire pig on a spit, roasting for hours until fork-tender. The Meat Club loves this recipe because it doesn't call for a spit! It's simply slow cooked on the stove top with a tangy barbecue sauce. This version, created by chef Erica Holland-Toll, is to die for! We love it on a ciabatta bun topped with coleslaw and apple slices.

SERVES 4

1 1/2 tablespoons olive oil

2 pounds pork top sirloin, cut into 1-inch cubes

2 cups water, plus more if needed

1 onion, diced

2 garlic cloves, crushed

2 tablespoons packed brown sugar

1/2 cup red wine vinegar

1 teaspoon salt

1/2 teaspoon Chinese hot chili sauce

1 cup ketchup

Salt

Freshly ground black pepper

1. Heat the oil in a large sauté pan or skillet over medium-high heat. Place the pork pieces in the pan and sauté until golden brown. Reduce the heat and add 1 1/2 cups of the water. Cover the pork and simmer on low heat until the water has evaporated and the meat is falling apart, approximately 1 hour. (The pork should easily pull apart with a fork; if not, add water as needed and continue cooking until tender.)

2. When tender, remove the meat from the pan and pour off all but 1 1/2 tablespoons of the fat that is left. Turn the heat back up to medium and add the onion and garlic. Scraping the bottom of the pan, cook until the onion and garlic are slightly golden brown, about 5 minutes. Stir in the brown sugar and cook until the sugar has melted.

3. Add the vinegar, salt, and chili sauce. Reduce the vinegar by half, stirring constantly so as to not let anything burn.

4. Add the ketchup and the remaining 1/2 cup water. Reduce the sauce slowly over medium-low heat until thick, about 15 minutes. Return the pork and any accumulated juices to the pan; stir vigorously to break up the pork. Taste and add salt and pepper as necessary. Serve immediately.

Apricot Chops

When Gemma moved to New York City, she had to get used to being without her meat girls. Lucky for her she has a sister, Elena, living in the city who was more than willing to eat meat with her. In keeping with the Wednesday night Meat Club on the West Coast, Gemma and Elena adopted "sister date night" on Wednesdays to cook and share their week's tales with each other. This meal was one of the creations that came out of date night—it is quick, easy, and oh-so-sweet! For this recipe, we recommend using the meatier rib chops, cut from the loin, which we enjoy cooked medium-rare.

SERVES 4

Four 1-inch-thick pork loin chops, preferably boneless, trimmed of excess fat

Salt

Freshly ground black pepper

1 tablespoon vegetable oil

1/4 cup chicken stock

1/2 cup apricot jam

1 tablespoon red wine vinegar

1 tablespoon minced shallot

1 tablespoon minced fresh thyme

2 teaspoons dry mustard

1. Preheat the oven to 450°F.

2. Season the pork chops with salt and pepper.

3. Heat a large, heavy, ovenproof sauté pan or skillet over high heat. Add the oil and heat until almost smoking. Add the pork chops to the skillet and sear about 2 minutes on each side.

4. In a small bowl, whisk together the stock, jam, vinegar, shallot, thyme, and mustard.

5. Top the chops with the sauce and transfer the pan into the oven. Bake for about 15 minutes, or until the meat is medium-rare and still juicy. Let rest for 5 minutes before serving.

F.E.B. Cutlets with Cranberry Chutney

F.E.B.—that's an acronym for flour, egg, and bread crumbs. A technique Vanessa picked up from watching her grandmother, it's the simplest way to remember how to bread anything from pork chops and veal cutlets to eggplant. Thinly sliced pork cutlets come from the sirloin end of the leg and are sometimes sold as pork scallops or scaloppine. They are fast, easy, and fun to cook for a small intimate dinner. The deep red Cranberry Chutney adds a saucy tartness that these chops can't resist! The chutney will keep, tightly sealed, for two weeks in the refrigerator.

SERVES 4

Cranberry Chutney

1 pound cranberries

2 cups sugar

½ cup water

½ cup fresh orange juice

2 teaspoons grated orange zest

1 teaspoon ground ginger

½ teaspoon ground cardamom

1. To make the Cranberry Chutney: Place all the ingredients in a medium saucepan over medium heat and cook, uncovered, until most of the cranberries pop open and the mixture is somewhat thickened, 7 to 10 minutes. Let cool to room temperature. (Makes about 3 cups.)

2. Meanwhile, make the cutlets: Place the flour, eggs, and bread crumbs in 3 separate shallow bowls.

3. Take 1 chop and dip it into the flour, then into the egg, then into the bread crumbs, so that at each step the chop is fully coated. Place the breaded chop on a platter and repeat with the remaining 3 chops.

F.E.B. Cutlets

1 1/2 cups flour

3 large eggs, lightly beaten

1 1/2 cups dried Italian flavored bread crumbs

Four 6-ounce pork loin, rib, or sirloin chops

2 tablespoons olive oil

1 teaspoon butter

Salt

Freshly ground black pepper

4. Heat the oil and butter in a sauté pan or skillet over medium heat. Place the chops in pan and brown for 5 to 8 minutes on each side, until cooked through. Season with salt and pepper to taste.

5. Keep warm in a low oven until ready to eat with the Cranberry Chutney.

Tangerine Dream Pork Chops

This was the first recipe that Kristina made in her new house when she moved out of San Francisco to the suburbs of Oakland. Vanessa and Gemma, who will gladly travel anywhere for meat, crossed the Bay Bridge and celebrated their friend's new adventure over this savory dish.

This recipe originally called for orange juice, but tangerine juice makes these chops a dream come true. Of course, if you don't have tangerine juice, any sweet citrus juice will do. The pancetta-shallot crust is a tasty treat and gives these chops just the right amount of crunch. We recommend serving these chops with a lightly dressed spring mix salad.

SERVES 4

Marinade

½ cup chopped onion

½ cup fresh tangerine juice

¼ cup olive oil

¼ cup fresh sage

¼ cup fresh parsley

1 tablespoon Dijon mustard

½ garlic clove, crushed

2 teaspoons tangerine zest

1 teaspoon honey

1. To make the marinade: In a large bowl, combine all the ingredients. Put the pork chops in the bowl and toss to coat all sides with the marinade. Cover and refrigerate for 4 hours or up to overnight.

2. To make the Pancetta-Shallot Crust: Cut the pancetta crosswise into thin strips. In a sauté pan or skillet over medium heat, cook until crisp; drain and set aside.

3. Preheat a grill to medium and the oven to 375°F. Heat the oil in a medium sauté pan or skillet over medium-high heat. Cook the shallots, stirring until caramelized, for about 5 minutes. Stir in the sugar and vinegar and cook until the sugar dissolves and the vinegar evaporates, about 2 minutes. Stir in the thyme, pepper, and pancetta and remove from the heat.

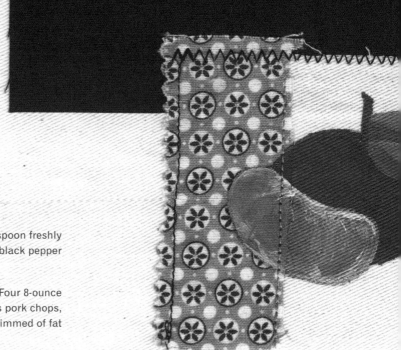

1 teaspoon freshly
ground black pepper

Four 8-ounce
boneless pork chops,
trimmed of fat

Pancetta-Shallot Crust

4 ounces pancetta,
cut 1/4 inch thick

1/2 tablespoon olive oil

1 cup thinly sliced shallots

1/2 tablespoon sugar

1/2 tablespoon
champagne vinegar

1/2 tablespoon
fresh thyme leaves

1 teaspoon freshly
ground black pepper

4. Wipe any excess marinade from the pork chops and discard the marinade. Grill the chops over direct heat, 2 to 3 minutes on each side, until well marked.

5. Place on a baking pan. Mound the pancetta-shallot mixture over the chops; bake for 15 to 20 minutes, until the top is crispy and the meat is cooked through. Serve immediately.

Simple Pork Chops with Greens 'n' Raisins

Savory pork chops on a bed of sautéed greens and sweet raisins is Southern-inspired fare. Our recipe calls for the bitter bite of mustard greens, but any greens will do—spinach, collard, or rainbow kale. You can also substitute black raisins, dried apricots, or other dried fruit for the golden raisins. We prefer pork loin chops for this recipe. Loin chops have a nice T-bone shape and include the loin muscle and some of the tenderloin. They are a bit leaner than rib chops, so watch your cooking time.

SERVES 4

5 strips thick-cut bacon

Four 1-inch-thick T-bone pork chops

Salt

Freshly ground black pepper

1 tablespoon olive oil, plus more if needed

¼ cup finely chopped onion

2 tablespoons chopped garlic

¼ cup beef stock

6 cups mustard greens

¼ cup golden raisins

1 tablespoon white wine vinegar

1. Place the bacon in a sauté pan or skillet over medium-high heat.

2. After about 4 minutes, turn the slices over and complete cooking on the other sides, until crispy.

3. Remove the bacon to a plate layered with paper towels to drain and cool. Chop into pieces.

4. Season the chops generously with salt and pepper.

5. In the pan you used for the bacon, heat the 1 tablespoon oil over high heat. Sear the chops on each side for 1 to 2 minutes, or until lightly browned. Reduce the heat to medium. Cover the pan and cook for 3 to 4 minutes on each side. The chops are done when the meat is firm to the touch; medium-rare chops will have a pink tinge.

6. Place the chops on a platter and keep the juices in the pan. Sauté the onion and garlic in the juices, adding a little more oil, if necessary. Cook until the onion is soft, approximately 5 minutes.

7. Stir in the stock, scraping up any browned
bits from the bottom of the pan, and add the
greens. Cook, covered, until the greens are
wilted, about 3 minutes. Stir in the raisins and
cook for 1 minute. Stir in the vinegar and toss
the greens to coat well. Add the chopped
bacon and toss. Add salt and pepper to taste.

8. Divide the greens among 4 plates and
serve the chops over the greens, spooning
juices over the top.

Patty Cakes

To make homemade sausages, you need a meat grinder and lots of time on your hands. The Meat Club loves the traditional method of making sausages but rarely has the luxury of time. We get our butcher to do the dirty work for us. Ask your butcher to grind up some pork butt for you (the premade sausages at your grocer are too lean and won't be as flavorful as the pork butt). All you'll have to do is add seasonings and pat them into shape.

We have two combinations of seasonings, depending on your mood. One is Eastern European–inspired, the other Moroccan. We love them both served with chunky applesauce and buttery mashed potatoes. Try to use *panko* (Japanese) bread crumbs instead of regular bread crumbs, as their consistency is lighter and not as dense.

SERVES 4

Mild Mood (Eastern European)

¼ cup panko bread crumbs

2 shallots, diced

3 tablespoons caraway seeds

2 tablespoons freshly ground black pepper

1½ tablespoons paprika

1½ tablespoons cayenne pepper

1 tablespoon salt

1. In a large bowl, mix well with a fork or by hand either the Mild Mood or Wild Mood seasoning combination with the ground pork.

2. Take one-quarter of the mixture and shape into an evenly round 4-inch patty. Repeat to make four patties.

3. Heat the oil in a large sauté pan or skillet over medium heat. Add the patties to the pan, leaving enough space between them to cook evenly. Cook over low to medium heat for 8 to 10 minutes per side, until golden brown and cooked through. Use a frying screen if you have it, to prevent hot grease from spattering. Serve hot.

Wild Mood (Moroccan)

1 small onion, diced

½ cup raisins

¼ cup ketchup

¼ cup panko bread crumbs

1 tablespoon curry powder

1 tablespoon ground allspice

1 tablespoon ground cumin

1 tablespoon ground cinnamon

1 tablespoon salt

1 tablespoon freshly
ground black pepper

2 pounds ground pork butt

3 tablespoons olive oil

BBCutie Spareribs

Fat and juicy, and plenty meaty, spareribs are the best. The secrets for great ribs on the grill are slow cooking and brushing on the sauce in the last few minutes of cooking. We give a recipe here for making our favorite barbecue sauce, but you are welcome to use your own home-made or bottled brand.

SERVES 4 TO 6

³/₄ cup chili powder

¹/₄ cup packed dark brown sugar

2 tablespoons coarsely ground black pepper

3¹/₂ teaspoons salt

1 tablespoon dried minced garlic

1 teaspoon onion powder

¹/₂ teaspoon ground cumin

3 sides pork spareribs (4 to 5 pounds)

1. In a small bowl, mix together the chili powder, brown sugar, pepper, salt, garlic, onion powder, and cumin.

2. Place the ribs on a baking sheet and rub with the mixture to fully coat. Cover and refrigerate for 2 to 4 hours.

3. Meanwhile, make the Barbecue Sauce: Heat the oil in a heavy medium saucepan over medium heat. Add the onion and sauté until tender, about 5 minutes. Add the garlic, paprika, and cayenne and stir for 1 minute. Add the ketchup, beer, vinegar, and Worcestershire sauce. Reduce the heat to medium-low. Simmer, uncovered, until the flavors blend and the sauce is slightly reduced, stirring occasionally, about 30 minutes. Meanwhile, prepare an outdoor grill for indirect heat (see page 20). Lightly oil the grate.

Barbecue Sauce

2 tablespoons vegetable oil

1 medium onion, finely chopped

2 tablespoons minced garlic

1 tablespoon paprika

1 teaspoon cayenne pepper

3/4 cup ketchup

1/2 cup beer

1/4 cup apple cider vinegar

1 tablespoon Worcestershire sauce

4. Cook the ribs, covered, for 2 hours, until the meat begins to pull away from the bones. Brush the ribs with the barbecue sauce during the last 5 to 10 minutes of cooking. Serve with more barbecue sauce for dipping. Pull up your sleeves and dig in!

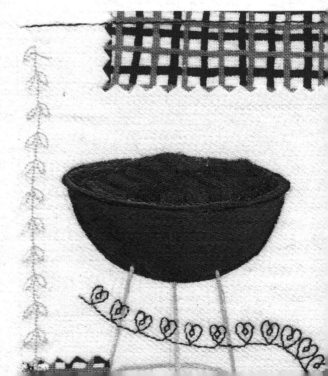

Best-Ever Ham

Mrs. Walsh, Gemma's family neighbor of forty years, first introduced this ham to Gemma at a holiday party. This dish then turned into the DePalma family's traditional Easter ham. Gemma updated the tradition by substituting apricots for the pineapple and adding a splash of amaretto. The Meat Club served this saucy rendition when they hosted an Oscar party for their friends. It was a hit, with enough leftovers for delicious ham sandwiches the next day. Use the butt end of a smoked ham for the best flavor.

SERVES 10

5- to 7-pound rump
(also called the butt end)
smoked ham

One 8-ounce can peeled apricots

1 cup packed brown sugar

1 cup plus 2 tablespoons amaretto

2 tablespoons fresh lemon juice

1 tablespoon dry mustard

1. Preheat the oven to 325°F.

2. Place the ham on a rack in a roasting pan, fat side up.

3. Drain the apricots, reserving ⅓ cup of the juice.

4. In a medium saucepan combine the reserved apricot juice, the brown sugar, the 1 cup of amaretto, the lemon juice, and the mustard. Bring to a boil.

5. Let the sauce cool slightly and spoon evenly all over the ham.

6. Bake the ham for 1 hour, basting every 20 minutes with sauce from the pan.

7. After an hour, top the ham with the apricots, using toothpicks to hold them in place, and splash the ham with the remaining 2 tablespoons amaretto.

8. Bake about 30 minutes longer, or until the ham and apricots are browned; a meat thermometer should read 140°F. Let rest for 5 minutes before slicing and serving.

Juicy Tidbit: Ham leftovers are great for sandwiches, topped with coleslaw on Italian bread.

Rigatoni with Spicy Sausage Sauce

This simple pasta dish provided Gemma with much comfort on her first night in a new apartment, with her new guy, in New York City. She made it for the Meat Club on a return visit. By definition, sausage is simply ground meat with seasoning and the variations are infinite! Vanessa recently discovered The Fatted Calf, an artisanal charcuterie specializing in hand-crafted, organic, and hormone-free meats (see Resources, page 133). Our Fatted Calf favorites include *boudin blanc,* finely ground veal and pork sausage, and the Fennel Italian-Style Pork Sausage.

SERVES 4

Four 2-ounce Italian sausages

2 tablespoons olive oil

1 yellow onion, chopped

4 garlic cloves, sliced

1 bulb fennel, thinly sliced

One 28-ounce can whole tomatoes, with their juices

2 tablespoons minced fresh basil

2 teaspoons red pepper flakes

Salt

Freshly ground black pepper

6 quarts water

1 pound rigatoni pasta

Grated Parmesan cheese for serving

1. Remove the sausages from their casings and sauté them in the oil in a skillet or sauté pan over medium heat until brown. Remove the meat and keep the oil in the pan.

2. Sauté the onion and garlic in the reserved oil until translucent, about 5 minutes. Add the fennel and sauté until soft, about 10 minutes.

3. Use your hands to crush the tomatoes and mix them into the sauté pan. Add the sausage, 1 tablespoon of the basil, and the red pepper flakes.

4. Simmer for 45 minutes over low heat, or until the sauce thickens and becomes rich. Season with salt and pepper.

5. Meanwhile, boil the water and add 2 tablespoons salt.

6. When water is at a rolling boil, add the pasta and cook until al dente, 8 to 10 minutes. Strain.

7. Divide the pasta among 4 plates, spoon the sauce over, and sprinkle with Parmesan cheese. Garnish with the remaining basil and enjoy!

Bacon, Basil, and Apple Sandwich

This is the Meat Club's take on the classic BLT. Though we love the BLT, we also are in love with the combination of pork and fruit. The salty bacon goes great with the sweet crispy apple. And the fresh basil is so much better than plain lettuce! You can use Canadian bacon for a leaner sandwich, but thick-cut American bacon does the job.

SERVES 3 TO 4

1 sweet French baguette

2 tablespoons mayonnaise

8 to 10 fresh basil leaves

15 slices thick-cut bacon, cooked

2 Fuji or Granny Smith apples, cored and thinly sliced

Salt

Freshly ground black pepper

1. Cut the baguette in half lengthwise.

2. Spread the mayo on both cut sides.

3. Start layering with the basil, bacon, and then the apple. Season with salt and pepper. Cut into servings and enjoy!

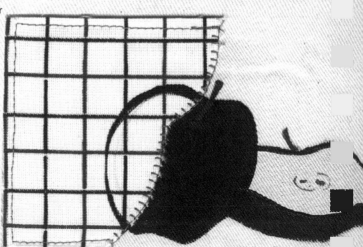

Chapter Four

Love Your Lamb!

Despite its small stature, lamb is large on our list. A little lamb chop or two makes for an intimate dinner, but we especially love to roast or braise a whole leg for a crowd. And believe us, a whole lamb leg is bigger than you think. Vanessa once bought a whole six-pound bone-in leg, not realizing just how heavy it would be. She was on foot and quite a ways from her apartment, so she had no choice but to call a cab in order to get it home!

For girls big on taste, lamb is the most flavorful of meats. Consequently, it doesn't need much to turn a cut into a masterpiece. A little salt and pepper on a tender chop or roast will give you a lovely meal. On the other hand, lamb's distinctive flavor stands up like no other to strong seasonings and spices, particularly garlic, rosemary, olives, fruit, and other ingredients found in Europe and the Mediterranean, where lamb is so popular. Over the years, we've created lamb dishes from the simple to the sublime, from rustic grilled chops over lemony bean salad to an elegant roasted rack of lamb to a sweet and spicy braised North African tagine.

Unlike beef and pork, most cuts of lamb are equally delicious, and whether you cook a chop, rib, or a roast, you'll be almost certain to have a tender and savory experience. Because of this, with the exception of the shank and the neck, almost all cuts of lamb can be grilled, broiled, roasted, or pan seared. Our favorite way to cook lamb is on the grill, because the flavor of lamb marries well with an open flame. No matter what the method, quick-cooked lamb chops, ribs, and roasts are best cooked rare or medium-rare.

Lamb also makes a magnificent stew or braise. Long-cooked lamb becomes lusciously tender and creates a marvelous sauce, especially when wine is involved. We've included recipes for braised lamb shanks, a lamb stew, and a leg of lamb that takes seven hours. Since these stews and braises are even better the next day, you can make them a day ahead. Whatever cut or style of meat you choose, we encourage you to love your lamb a long time!

The Meaty Basics: Lamb

Making the Grade

The four grades of lamb are prime, choice, good, and utility. You won't see much prime or utility meat and, like pork and beef, most lamb is choice grade.

You've Got the Look

Look for lamb that is moist and bright, with a color that ranges from pinkish rose to light red. Lamb doesn't need a lot of marbling to be tender. The meat should be fine textured, with smooth white fat, and bones that are reddish and moist. The lamb should smell fresh. Avoid meat that is dark purple and has dry white bones.

Favorite Flavorings

We love to slather, marinate, stew, and sauce lamb with such sweet and savory ingredients as garlic, mustard, cumin, curry, oregano, fennel, prunes, cherries, feta cheese, rosemary, pepper, mint, olives, tarragon, capers, aromatic vegetables, wine, coriander, and cilantro.

Cook It Right

For most cuts, we love our lamb cooked rare to medium-rare so that the meat is red and rosy when pricked with a knife or when its temperature registers 120°F on an instant-read thermometer. Since most lamb is young and tender, almost any cut (chops, ribs, or roasts) can be cooked by most dry heat methods—grilling, roasting, broiling. We like to quick-cook our chops under the broiler or on the stove. Center-cut loin roasts and leg roasts are tasty butterflied and cooked on a charcoal grill or whole in the oven. Tougher cuts such as the shanks and the sinewy shoulder are delicious braised and stewed.

Storage

Store fresh lamb well-wrapped two to four days in the refrigerator and up to six months in the freezer.

The Mystique of the Lamb Physique

Lamb includes five primal cuts (see figure on fold-out): shoulder, ribs, loin, leg, and shank/breast (also known as the foreleg).

SHOULDER: Fatty and flavorful, cuts from the shoulder are wonderful for roasting, braising, and stewing. The high fat content makes it less suited for grilling, unless you like flare-ups! Shoulders are sold whole or in pieces, with the bone in or out; boneless shoulders are easier to cut into chunks. Meat from this area should be cooked to the medium to well-done stage. The shoulder includes shoulder chops and square-cut shoulder chops that are sinewy but very flavorful and are best used to make hearty stews.

RIBS: This section includes some of the most tender and tasty cuts of lamb, including the lovely and luxurious rack of lamb that can also be cut into chops. The rib chops have a nice "eye of meat" that is soft and juicy because of its high fat content. The thicker double lamb chops (which are doubly good in our opinion) are cut from both sides of the backbone.

LOIN: The luscious loin includes the most tender and juicy chops and roasts. The loin can be sold whole as the saddle or cut up into T-bone-shaped chops, as it is usually found. We love loin chops because they are tender and not as fatty as the rib chops. Our favorite roasts from the loin include the luscious and elegant whole loin of lamb and the lamb tenderloin. Boneless loin (almost always) can be cut into medallions and quickly cooked.

LEG: Lambs are known for their great legs, and meat from the leg makes excellent roasts, braises, stews, and even steaks. Meat from the leg is sold whole or in halves, boned or bone in, cubed, or ground for stews or kebabs. We love to roast or braise a whole leg for a crowd of six or more. Half legs are sold as the shank end (which is less meaty) and the sirloin end (which is more meaty and tender). As an alternative to quick-cooked chops, we love steaks cut from the sirloin end of the leg. These leg steaks are very meaty, relatively cheap, and are delicious grilled or broiled or used in a stew.

SHANK/BREAST/FORELEG: Inexpensive shanks are tough but are completely transformed with a simple braise. To us, nothing beats the silken texture of a braised lamb shank. Spoil yourself with Shanks for the Memories (page 124), slow-cooked in a rich wine sauce, on a cold winter's night.

There is so much lamb and so little time! We hope you, too, fall easily in love with lamb as we have.

Tarted-Up Lamb Steaks with Cherries

For all you little tarts out there, here's a springtime recipe that features the luscious sweetness and color of summertime cherries. The bone-in lamb leg steak resembles a bone-in sirloin. We recommend using Bing cherries, but if you can't find them, choose the darkest, sweetest cherries available.

SERVES 4

5 tablespoons olive oil

4 large shallots, thinly sliced

¼ cup coarsely chopped flat-leaf parsley

12 to 15 fresh or dried pitted cherries

Salt

Freshly ground black pepper

Four 6- to 7-ounce bone-in lamb leg steaks, cut ½ inch thick

1. In a large skillet or sauté pan, heat 1 tablespoon of the oil over high heat. Add the shallots and sauté, stirring, until the shallots have just softened, about 1 minute. Transfer the shallots to a small bowl.

2. Stir in 3 more tablespoons of the oil, the parsley, and the cherries.

3. Season the mixture with salt and pepper, transfer to a serving bowl, and set aside.

4. Season the lamb steaks with salt and pepper.

5. In the same skillet, heat the remaining 1 tablespoon oil over high heat. Add the lamb steaks and cook until well browned, 4 to 5 minutes on each side. Transfer the lamb steaks to a platter to rest for 5 minutes, then serve with the cherry relish.

Charming Lamb Chops with Charmoula Sauce

Made with fresh herbs, *charmoula*, a bright green, lemony, cumin-scented, Moroccan sauce, is a snap to make and drizzle over these darling little chops. We recommend using rib chops for this recipe because they are meaty, tender, tasty, and match well with the sauce. *Charmoula* is also delicious the next day and can be enjoyed as a dip, spread, or garnish.

SERVES 4

Salt

Freshly ground black pepper

8 lamb rib chops

Charmoula Sauce

1/2 cup fresh cilantro, chopped

1/2 cup fresh flat-leaf parsley, chopped

1/2 cup olive oil

5 garlic cloves, crushed

1/3 cup fresh lemon juice

2 teaspoons coriander

2 teaspoons paprika

2 teaspoons salt

1 1/2 teaspoons ground cumin

1/4 teaspoon red pepper flakes

1. Salt and pepper the chops and set aside to come to room temperature.

2. To make the *Charmoula* Sauce: Puree all the ingredients in a food processor or blender.

3. Set the oven to broil and put an oven rack on the top shelf.

4. Place the chops in a shallow baking dish and pour the sauce over the chops. Broil 4 minutes per side, until the chops are golden. Let rest for 5 minutes before serving. Save some sauce on the side for dipping!

Lamb Chops and Turnip Mash

We usually love our chops with mashed potatoes, but we ran out once and turnips saved the day. The sweet, earthy flavor of turnips takes us back to our European roots and stands up well to double-thick rib chops. Though this combination was unplanned, the results were surprisingly tasty. The Meat Club got off to a late start and this dish was whipped up in minutes. Double-thick rib chops are also known as English-cut lamb chops. Cut from the rib, double-thick lamb chops are tender and juicy and are terrific cooked rare.

SERVES 4

4 white round or
Yukon Gold potatoes,
peeled and chopped
into 1/2-inch pieces

3 turnips,
peeled and chopped
into 1/2-inch pieces

1/4 cup cream

3 tablespoons unsalted butter

Salt

Freshly ground black pepper

1/4 cup chopped fresh
flat-leaf parsley

3 tablespoons
dried bread crumbs

4 double-thick lamb rib chops

2 tablespoons olive oil

1. Place the potatoes and turnips in a saucepan. Cover with water and boil for 10 to 15 minutes, until soft.

2. Remove from the heat. Add the cream, butter, and salt and pepper to taste and mash until smooth and creamy. Let sit over low heat until the chops are ready to serve.

3. Preheat the broiler. Mix the parsley and bread crumbs in a small bowl.

4. Lay the chops on a broiling pan and brush with the oil. Season each side with salt and pepper, then pat on the bread-crumb mixture to coat evenly.

5. Broil for 5 to 7 minutes on each side, until golden. Remove from the oven and let rest for 4 to 5 minutes before serving with the turnip mash.

Li'l Lamb Chops with Lemon and White Bean Salad

No need to bust your chops in the kitchen with this recipe. We love to use the leaner loin chops for this recipe, but rib chops work just as well. Served over the White Bean Salad, the lemon dressing screams with flavor. Kick back and enjoy a lemon drop cocktail while the chops are marinating!

SERVES 6

Marinade

⅓ cup olive oil

Juice of 2 lemons

5 cloves garlic, minced

1 teaspoon salt

½ teaspoon freshly ground black pepper

¼ teaspoon dried oregano

6 (about 4 pounds) lamb loin or rib chops (1 inch thick)

1. To make the marinade: In a small bowl, mix all the ingredients.

2. Rub the marinade over the lamb, place the lamb in a large, self-sealing plastic bag, and marinate for 2 hours at room temperature or overnight in the refrigerator.

3. To make the dressing: In a food processor, blend together the lemon juice, water, lemon zest, vinegar, oregano, garlic, and pepper until smooth. While the processor is running, add the oil, blending to make a homogenous dressing. Pour the dressing into a small bowl.

4. To make the White Bean Salad: Mix the beans, onion, tomatoes, and olives in a large bowl. Toss with the dressing and place on a platter. Sprinkle the feta cheese over the salad. Set aside.

Dressing

Juice of 2 lemons

2 tablespoons water

2 tablespoons lemon zest

1½ tablespoons
red wine vinegar

2 teaspoons dried oregano

2 teaspoons crushed
or minced garlic

½ teaspoon freshly
ground black pepper

¼ cup olive oil

White Bean Salad

2 cups cooked or
drained canned
white beans (cannellini
or great Northern)

1 cup cooked or
drained canned
garbanzo beans

1 medium red onion,
finely diced

8 ounces cherry
tomatoes, halved

½ cup pitted black
or green olives

½ cup (4 ounces)
crumbled feta cheese

5. Preheat the broiler or grill, and cook the chops 3 inches from the flame for 3 to 5 minutes per side. The chops should register 120° to 132°F at the thickest part for rare to medium-rare. Let the meat rest for at least 5 minutes before serving.

6. Divide the salad among plates and top each with a chop.

Post-Date Lamb Chops with Mint Aioli

Ever come home from a date hungry? This simple dish was inspired by an unsuccessful first (and last) date who insisted on splitting a measly chicken breast! Needless to say our Meat Club girl went home hungry, but the less-than-juicy tale was worth sharing with the gals. When broiling quick-cooking items such as chops, turn them only once. If you leave the meat alone for a few minutes, it will have a chance to form a nice brown crust. The Mint Aioli is also delicious spread on crusty bread.

SERVES 4

Mint Aioli

1 large garlic clove, minced

¼ cup fresh mint, julienned

1 cup mayonnaise

¼ cup extra-virgin olive oil

1 tablespoon fresh lemon juice

Salt

Freshly ground black pepper

1. To make the Mint Aioli: In a food processor, combine the garlic and mint and pulse to puree.

2. Add the mayonnaise and process until smooth.

3. With the machine on, gradually add the extra-virgin oil and process until emulsified.

4. Scrape the aioli into a bowl, stir in the lemon juice, and season with salt and pepper.

5. Store in a tightly sealed container in the refrigerator for up to 2 weeks. (Makes about 1¼ cups.)

Lamb chops

6 tablespoons olive oil

2 garlic cloves, minced

4 teaspoons chopped
fresh rosemary

1/2 teaspoon salt

1/4 teaspoon freshly
ground black pepper

8 lamb rib chops,
about 1 inch thick
(about 2 3/4 pounds in all)

6. To make the lamb chops, preheat the broiler. In a shallow dish, combine 4 table-spoons of the olive oil with the garlic, rose-mary, salt, and pepper. Add the lamb chops and turn to coat.

7. Broil the lamb chops on the first side for 5 minutes, basting with the remaining 2 tablespoons olive oil. Turn and cook on the second side until golden, about 5 minutes longer. Let rest for 5 minutes, then serve with the Mint Aioli.

Crown Roast

The crown roast is a reason for celebration. There are so many varieties out there. Ours is pretty simple: tender lamb with potatoes and Gruyère—what could be better? The crown roast is elegant in appearance. Get your butcher to tie the lamb racks into a crown and be sure to cover the ends of the bones with aluminum foil before roasting so they don't burn. After cooking, you can decorate with a girly touch by adding decorative pink paper ends!

SERVES 4 TO 6

2 lamb racks, tied into a crown roast

Salt

Freshly ground black pepper

5 large potatoes

1 pound pancetta, diced

1 large onion, chopped

2 garlic cloves, minced

1 cup (8 ounces) grated Swiss Gruyère cheese

¼ cup grated Parmesan cheese

¼ cup fresh flat-leaf parsley

¼ cup fresh basil

1. Preheat the oven to 375°F.

2. Sprinkle the crown roast lightly with salt and pepper and place in a large roasting pan. Roast for 30 minutes.

3. Meanwhile, peel and grate the potatoes.

4. Fry the diced pancetta slowly in a heavy skillet over medium-low heat. When crisp, pour off any excess fat, add the onion and garlic, and sauté until translucent.

5. Stir in the potatoes and add pepper to taste. Sauté slowly over low heat for 25 to 30 minutes, stirring frequently to prevent burning. The potatoes should be dry and lightly browned. Remove from the heat and mix in the cheeses, parsley, and basil. Stir until the cheese melts and add salt to taste.

6. After the roast has baked for 30 minutes, heap the potato mixture into the center of the crown roast. Roast for 30 minutes longer, or until the stuffing is golden brown and the meat is medium-rare. Let rest for 10 minutes before cutting the roast into servings.

Sugar 'n' Spice Lamb

This recipe originated from a close gal-pal of ours. It was originally made with chicken, but the Meat Club fancied a richer flavor. Lamb shoulder did the job. Lamb shoulder is very tender when braised for a few hours. Marinate the lamb overnight for a truly sumptuous experience.

SERVES 4

Four 8-ounce lamb shoulder steaks

1/2 cup soy sauce

1/2 cup sweet Marsala wine

2 tablespoons minced garlic

4 teaspoons ground cumin

2 teaspoons smoked paprika

6 tablespoons olive oil

2 large onions, chopped

2 tablespoons flour

4 teaspoons ground cinnamon

1 teaspoon cayenne pepper

2 teaspoons kosher salt

1 tablespoon butter

3 cups chicken stock

1/4 cup brown sugar

1 cup peeled 1-inch carrot pieces

Cooked couscous (optional)

2 lemons, sliced into rounds

1. Place the lamb steaks in a baking dish or large, heavy-duty self-sealing plastic bag. Combine the soy sauce, Marsala, garlic, cumin, paprika, and 3 tablespoons of the oil in a small bowl. Pour the mixture over the lamb steaks and refrigerate, covered, overnight.

2. Heat the remaining 3 tablespoons of olive oil in a Dutch oven over medium heat. Sauté the onions until they are translucent and soft. Remove from the Dutch oven with a slotted spoon and set aside. Leave the pot on the heat.

3. In a small bowl, mix the flour, cinnamon, cayenne, and salt. Take the steaks out of the marinade and coat them in the flour mixture. Save the marinade for braising.

4. Melt the butter in the Dutch oven and brown the lamb steaks. Once the steaks are browned on all sides, pour the reserved marinade, the stock, and the cooked onions over top, stirring to incorporate any browned bits from the bottom of pan. The liquid should cover the lamb halfway.

5. Braise, covered, on the stove top over low to medium heat for 2 to 3 hours, until fork-tender. Add the brown sugar and carrots during the last hour of cooking. Serve over couscous with the lemon slices.

Heavenly Leg of Lamb with Baked Apples

If Eve had known how good these fruit-stuffed baked apples were, she might have prepared them this way before she tempted Adam. Be aware that a five-pound leg of lamb is a huge piece of meat. When Vanessa bought a leg this big, it was so heavy she had to take a cab to get it home. For a make-ahead meal, marinate the lamb and prepare the apples the night before. The next day, you can just reheat the apples while the lamb is cooking.

SERVES 6

Herb-Coated Leg of Lamb

1/2 garlic head, cloves peeled

1/4 cup olive oil

3 teaspoons whole-grain Dijon mustard

2 teaspoons fresh rosemary

2 teaspoons fresh thyme leaves

1 1/2 teaspoons ground coriander

1 teaspoon cayenne pepper

1 bay leaf

Freshly ground black pepper

One 5-pound leg of lamb, butterflied

1. To prepare the lamb: In a food processor, combine the garlic, oil, mustard, rosemary, thyme, coriander, cayenne, bay leaf, and pepper to taste. Puree into a paste.

2. Place the lamb in a 9-by-13-inch glass baking dish and rub with the paste. Cover and refrigerate overnight.

3. To make the baked apples: 1 1/2 hours before you want to eat, preheat the oven to 400°F. Combine the raisins, dates, walnuts, brown sugar, and cinnamon in a small bowl. Place the apples in a 9-by-13-inch baking dish. Fill the apples with the date mixture.

4. Combine the water, brandy, and melted butter in a small bowl. Pour over the apples. Cover and bake, basting occasionally with the sauce, until the apples are tender, about 1 1/4 hours. Set aside.

Fruit-Stuffed Baked Apples

¼ cup raisins

6 pitted dates or prunes, sliced

¼ cup chopped walnuts

2 teaspoons packed
brown sugar

1 teaspoon ground cinnamon

6 apples,
cored and tops peeled

¼ cup water

¼ cup brandy

4 tablespoons (½ stick)
unsalted butter, melted

5. Meanwhile, preheat a grill to medium heat. Grill the lamb over direct heat for 15 to 20 minutes per side for rare, or longer if you like it more well done. Transfer to a large platter and cover with foil. Let stand for 10 minutes before slicing the lamb across the grain. Serve with the apples and enjoy!

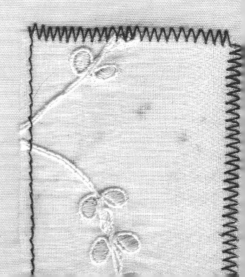

Citrus-Scented Lamb Tagine

Traditional tagines, the wonderfully spicy North African stews, are typically cooked for hours in clay or ceramic pots. We found that a cast-iron enameled casserole worked just as well for this recipe and cut the cooking time to fifty minutes. Boneless lamb shoulder roast is the best cut to use for this recipe, but if you can only find bone-in shoulder meat, also known as square-cut lamb shoulder roast, have your butcher cut the meat up for you. The dish is even better after it sits in the fridge overnight topped with freshly grated citrus zest.

SERVES 4

2 pounds lean boneless lamb shoulder and neck, cut into 1-inch pieces

Salt

Freshly ground black pepper

3 tablespoons unsalted butter

4 medium carrots, peeled and sliced

1 medium onion, finely chopped

1 tablespoon minced fresh cilantro, plus a few leaves for garnish

1 tablespoon grated peeled fresh ginger

1. Season the lamb with salt and pepper.

2. Melt the butter in an enameled cast-iron casserole. Add the lamb to the casserole and brown on all sides over medium-high heat, about 10 minutes. Transfer the meat to a large plate.

3. Add the carrots and onion to the casserole and sauté over medium heat until softened, about 10 minutes. Return the meat to the casserole. Add the cilantro, ginger, lemon and orange zest strips, cinnamon, allspice, and salt and pepper to taste, stirring until fragrant. Add the tomatoes and juice and the stock and bring the stew to a boil.

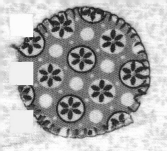

Three 3-inch strips
lemon zest, plus grated
zest for garnish

Three 3-inch strips
orange zest, plus grated
zest for garnish

¼ teaspoon
ground cinnamon

¼ teaspoon
ground allspice

One 8-ounce can diced
tomatoes, with their juices

½ cup chicken stock

One 10-ounce package
frozen baby peas

4. Cook over medium heat, partially covered, until the meat is tender, about 50 minutes. Stir in the peas and cook, uncovered, until the sauce thickens, about 10 minutes more. Serve with finely grated lemon and orange zest and cilantro on top.

Shanks for the Memories

After Gemma moved to New York City, she tried a few recipes that did not work. She had a serious case of meat defeat and was thinking of returning to her vegetarian ways. A trip to California and a Meat meeting with the girls that included kitchen coaching and support cured her! Gemma made this memorable lamb shank recipe at Kristina's house and was met with great success. A good crusty Italian bread is a must with this meal to soak up all the savory juices.

SERVES 8

Four 1-pound lamb shanks

2 tablespoons salt

1 tablespoon freshly ground black pepper

3 tablespoons canola oil

1 onion, coarsely chopped

2 carrots, peeled and cut into 1/2-inch pieces

1 large stalk celery, cut into 1/2-inch pieces

1 leek, white parts only, cut into 1-inch pieces

4 garlic cloves, minced

2 tablespoons tomato paste

2 tablespoons fresh thyme

1. Preheat the oven to 325°F.

2. Season the shanks with the salt and pepper.

3. In an ovenproof roasting pan or Dutch oven, heat the canola oil over high heat.

4. Working in batches, brown the shanks 4 minutes per side. Transfer the shanks to a plate and set aside.

5. Add the onion, carrots, celery, leek, and minced garlic to the pan. Sauté, stirring constantly, until softened, about 10 minutes.

6. Stir in the tomato paste, coating the vegetables completely.

7. Return the shanks to the pan with the vegetables. Add half of the thyme and half of the tarragon. Add the stock to cover the shanks and bring to a simmer.

8. Partially cover the pan with aluminum foil and place in the oven. Braise for about 3 hours, or until the meat pulls easily from the bone. Remove the pan from the oven and transfer the shanks to a plate.

4 tablespoons
fresh tarragon

4 cups chicken stock

1 garlic head

3 tablespoons olive oil

One 8-ounce can
fire-roasted tomatoes

Two 8-ounce cans
navy beans,
drained and rinsed

2 bunches fresh arugula

9. Meanwhile, cut off the top of the head of garlic so the cloves are exposed. Drizzle the olive oil over the garlic on a sheet of aluminum foil and bake for 45 minutes, until the garlic becomes browned on top. The garlic should be soft enough to simply squeeze out of the cloves.

10. Strain the braising liquid, discarding the solids. Return the liquid to the pan and bring to a simmer.

11. Return the shanks to the reduced liquid and add the roasted tomatoes and the roasted garlic squeezed from the cloves.

12. Simmer over medium heat until the broth has reduced by one-third, about 10 minutes.

13. Stir in the beans and the remaining thyme and tarragon. Add the arugula and cook until just wilted. Serve immediately.

Mustard and Mint-Crusted Rack of Lamb

One of our mottos in the Meat Club is, "Butter always makes it better!" The secret to this recipe is a mint-butter compound, which when slathered over the rack of lamb makes a scrumptious crust. An elegant and delicious roast, the rack of lamb makes for impressive dinner party fare. A trimmed rack of lamb, ready for the oven, is called *frenched*. We have our butcher do all the trimming. Kristina made this recipe with fresh mint from her garden. Mint is easy to grow and is a versatile herb; add sprigs to fresh lemonade or make mojitos.

SERVES 8

1½ cups fresh bread crumbs

3 tablespoons finely chopped fresh flat-leaf parsley

2 tablespoons finely chopped fresh mint

1½ teaspoons minced fresh rosemary

Salt

1. In a small bowl, stir together the bread crumbs, parsley, 1 tablespoon of the mint, the rosemary, ½ teaspoon salt, and ¼ teaspoon pepper, then drizzle with 2½ tablespoons of the oil.

2. In another small bowl, mix together the remaining 1 tablespoon mint with the butter to create a mint-butter compound.

3. Put an oven rack in the middle position and preheat to 400°F.

4. Season the lamb with salt and pepper. Heat the remaining 1 tablespoon oil in a large heavy skillet or sauté pan over medium-high heat until hot but not smoking. Brown the lamb 1 rack at a time, turning once, about 4 minutes per rack. Transfer to a 13-by-9-by-2-inch roasting pan, arranging fatty sides up.

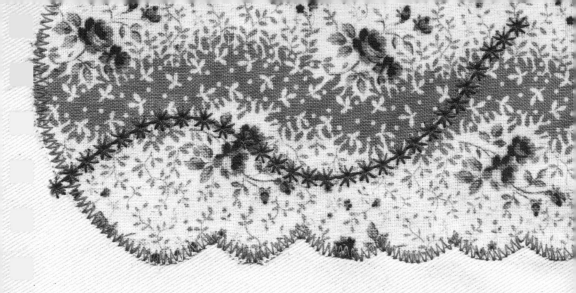

Freshly ground black pepper

3½ tablespoons olive oil

3 tablespoons unsalted
butter, softened

Three 1-pound
frenched lamb racks,
trimmed of most fat

2 tablespoons Dijon mustard

3 garlic cloves, minced

5. Spread the fatty sides of each rack with the mustard and garlic. Divide the bread crumb mixture into 3 portions and pat each portion over the mustard-garlic coating on each rack, gently pressing to adhere. Divide the mint-butter compound into 3 equal parts and place each portion on top of the bread-crumb mixture of each rack.

6. Roast the lamb until an instant-read thermometer inserted diagonally 2 inches into the center (do not touch bone) registers 130°F for medium-rare, 20 to 25 minutes, and transfer to a cutting board.

7. Let rest for 10 minutes, then cut into chops and serve them up.

Confetti Lamb Kebabs

Traditionally a Turkish method of cooking, kebab means "roasted meat." Nomadic Turks would sit around a campfire and roast their meat for dinner. Kebabs are fun to create, beautiful to behold, and delicious to eat. We prefer the flavor and tenderness of boneless leg of lamb for our kebabs, but you can use a less expensive cut from the sirloin or shoulder. Threaded on very short 4-inch skewers (instead of 8-inch skewers), these fun, colorful sticks are perfect for passing at parties. As with all kebabs, these take some preparation, so make sure to give yourself time to boil the sweet potatoes and pearl onions.

SERVES 8

1 tablespoon soy sauce

1 tablespoon fresh lemon juice

1 tablespoon sugar

One 4-pound leg of lamb, cut into 1-inch cubes (about 36)

36 four-inch wooden skewers

1 medium sweet potato, peeled and cut into ¾-inch cubes

1. In a large bowl, combine the soy sauce, lemon juice, and sugar. Add the lamb and toss until well coated. Cover and refrigerate for 1 hour.

2. Meanwhile, soak the wooden skewers in water for about 1 hour.

3. Bring a pot of salted water to a boil and add the sweet potato cubes. Boil for about 5 minutes, or until tender. Remove the potato cubes with a slotted spoon and rinse under cold water. Put into a bowl and set aside.

4. In the same pot of boiling water, add the pearl onions and cook for 1 minute. Drain, peel, and set aside.

5. Preheat a grill to medium heat.

6. In a large bowl, stir together the paprika, cumin, salt, and cinnamon. Drain the lamb in a colander, reserving the marinade, and pat dry. Add the lamb to the spices and toss to coat.

2 pounds pearl onions

1 teaspoon paprika

1 teaspoon ground cumin

1 teaspoon salt

1/4 teaspoon ground cinnamon

2 red bell peppers,
cut into 1-inch pieces

7. On each skewer, thread alternating pieces of sweet potato, lamb, bell pepper, and pearl onions. Arrange the kebabs on the grill and cook over direct heat for 8 to 10 minutes, turning the skewers occasionally. If the meat looks as if it is drying out, baste with the reserved marinade as needed. The lamb should be pink in the middle and the vegetables should be nicely marked by the grill. Serve immediately.

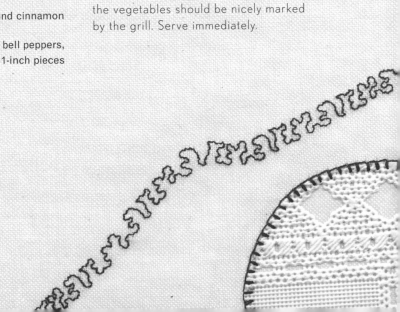

Lamb Sloppy Janes

This is our answer to the Sloppy Joe, a robust dish that is typically made with beef. We found that after an hour of baking time, the lamb flavor is incredible. It beats those tired Sloppy Joes with the heavy tomato sauce that we all grew up with. We think of our version as a mini moussaka—the popular Middle Eastern dish. Make this the night before and serve it up for a casual Friday night dinner.

SERVES 4 TO 6

2 globe eggplants

Salt

2 tablespoons olive oil

1 onion, cut into medium dice

Freshly ground black pepper

1 teaspoon dried oregano

1 teaspoon ground cinnamon

1 teaspoon ground cumin

1/4 teaspoon cayenne pepper

1 1/4 pounds ground lamb
(see headnote, page 132)

1. Using a sharp knife, slice the eggplants into 1/4-inch rounds. Salt the eggplant slices generously and let them drain in a colander for 30 minutes. Rinse the slices and pat them dry with paper towels.

2. Preheat the oven to 350°F.

3. In a large skillet or sauté pan, heat the oil over high heat. Add the onion and sauté until softened, about 10 minutes. Season with salt and pepper.

4. Add the oregano, cinnamon, cumin, and cayenne and cook for about 2 more minutes, until the mixture is fragrant with spice.

5. Add the lamb and cook for about 8 minutes, or until browned. Drain off the fat, add the tomatoes, and cook over medium heat until the sauce starts to thicken, about 10 minutes.

6. Place the eggplant slices on a rimmed baking sheet and top with about one-third of the sauce.

One 28-ounce can diced tomatoes, drained

1 tablespoon chopped fresh flat-leaf parsley, plus extra for garnish

1 tablespoon dried bread crumbs

7. Repeat this layering twice to make 3-layer stacks.

8. Combine the 1 tablespoon parsley and the bread crumbs and sprinkle over the top.

9. Cover with foil and bake for 1 hour.

10. Remove the foil and place under the broiler or bake for 10 minutes more, until browned.

11. Sprinkle more parsley over the top and serve.

Lamb Curry in a Hurry

Lamb curry is one of Kristina's favorite dishes to order in Indian restaurants. She never considered making it at home until her daughter was born and her evenings out came to a halt. Packaged ground lamb can be difficult to find. We recommend that you buy a piece of the leg or the shoulder and have your butcher grind it up for you.

SERVES 4

2 tablespoons vegetable oil

1 medium onion, coarsely chopped

2 garlic cloves, minced

1 tablespoon minced
peeled fresh ginger

1½ pounds ground lamb,
preferably lean

1½ tablespoons curry powder

1 medium sweet potato,
peeled and cut into ½-inch dice

One 14-ounce can coconut milk

1 cup chicken stock

Salt

Freshly ground black pepper

½ cup thawed frozen baby peas

½ cup drained canned garbanzo beans

⅓ cup coarsely chopped fresh cilantro

Cooked basmati rice for serving

Hot sauce (optional)

1. In a large, deep skillet, heat the oil until hot. Add the onion, garlic, and ginger and cook over medium-high heat until soft, about 4 minutes. Add the lamb and cook, breaking it up with a wooden spoon, until it starts to brown, about 10 minutes.

2. Add the curry powder and sweet potato and cook for 2 minutes.

3. Add the coconut milk and stock and season with salt and pepper. Cover partially and simmer over medium heat until the sweet potato is tender, about 15 minutes.

4. Add the peas and garbanzo beans and cook until heated through.

5. Stir in the cilantro and serve over basmati rice with hot sauce, if desired.

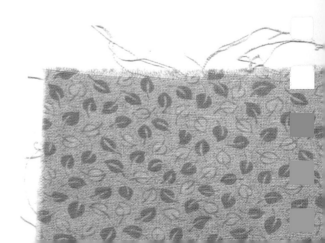

Resources

Coleman Natural Meats
800-442-8666
www.colemannatural.com
coleman@colemannatural.com

Producers of good-tasting, high-quality
meats through sustainable methods.

Fatted Calf Charcuterie
510-301-9279
Fax: 510-653-4327

Delicious selection of artisanal
charcuterie from pâtés to fresh
homemade sausages.

Meyer Natural
800 Cattail Road
Lincoln, NE 68521
800-856-6765
www.meyernaturalangus.com

Excellent purveyor of Angus beef
products sold in the United States
and abroad.

Niman Ranch
510-808-0340
www.nimanranch.com

Produces the finest-tasting,
hormone-free, natural-fed meat
in the world.

Organic Valley
CROPP Cooperative
507 West Main Street
LaFarge, WI 54639
888-444-6455
Fax: 608-625-2600
www.organicvalley.coop

The largest organic farmer-owner
cooperative in North America.

Potter Family Farms
One Ferry Building (Embarcadero)
Shop #32
San Francisco, CA 94111
415-378-2917
530-902-7055
www.potterfamilyfarms.com

Dry-aged, artisan-quality, homegrown
meats raised with environmental
awareness.

Index

Table of Equivalents

The exact equivalents in the following tables
have been rounded for convenience.

Liquid/Dry Measures

U.S.	Metric
1/4 teaspoon	1.25 milliliters
1/2 teaspoon	2.5 milliliters
1 teaspoon	5 milliliters
1 tablespoon (3 tsp)	15 milliliters
1 fluid ounce (2 tbs)	30 milliliters
1/4 cup	60 milliliters
1/3 cup	80 milliliters
1/2 cup	120 milliliters
1 cup	240 milliliters
1 pint (2 cups)	480 milliliters
1 quart (4 cups, 32 oz)	960 milliliters
1 gallon (4 quarts)	3.84 liters
1 ounce (by weight)	28 grams
1 pound	454 grams
2.2 pounds	1 kilogram

Length

U.S.	Metric
1/8 inch	3 millimeters
1/4 inch	6 millimeters
1/2 inch	12 millimeters
1 inch	2.5 centimeters

Oven Temperature

Fahrenheit	Celsius	Gas
250	120	1/2
275	140	1
300	150	2
325	160	3
350	180	4
375	190	5
400	200	6
425	220	7
450	230	8
475	240	9
500	260	10